Legal System

Other Books of Related Interest:

Opposing Viewpoints Series

The Patriot Act

Current Controversies Series

Capital Punishment

Drug Legalization

At Issue Series

Alternatives to Prisons

Are Privacy Rights Being Violated?

Does Capital Punishment Deter Crime?

How Should Prisons Treat Inmates?

How Should the United States Treat Prisoners in the War on Terror?

Legalizing Drugs

"Congress shall make
no law . . . abridging
the freedom of speech,
or of the press."

First Amendment to the U.S. Constitution

The basic foundation of our democracy is the First Amendment guarantee of freedom of expression. The Opposing Viewpoints Series is dedicated to the concept of this basic freedom and the idea that it is more important to practice it than to enshrine it.

Legal System

Clare Hanrahan, Book Editor

GREENHAVEN PRESS

An imprint of Thomson Gale, a part of The Thomson Corporation

Detroit • New York • San Francisco • New Haven, Conn. • Waterville, Maine • London

Christine Nasso, *Publisher*
Elizabeth Des Chenes, *Managing Editor*

© 2008 The Gale Group.

Star logo is a trademark and Gale and Greenhaven Press are registered trademarks used herein under license.

For more information, contact:
Greenhaven Press
27500 Drake Rd.
Farmington Hills, MI 48331-3535
Or you can visit our Internet site at http://www.gale.com

LIBRARY OF CONGRESS CATALOGING-IN-PUBLICATION DATA

Legal System / Clare Hanrahan, book editor.
   p. cm. -- (Opposing viewpoints)
   Includes bibliographical references and index.
   ISBN-13: 978-0-7377-3757-8 (hardcover)
   ISBN-13: 978-0-7377-3758-5 (pbk.)
   1. Justice, Administration of--United States--Popular works. 2. Jury--United States--Popular works. 3. Television broadcasting of court proceedings--United States--Popular works. I. Hanrahan, Clare.
   KF8700.Z9L43 2008
   347.73--dc22
                                                                    2007032718

ISBN-10: 0-7377-3757-3 (hardcover)
ISBN-10: 0-7377-3758-1 (pbk.)

Printed in the United States of America
10 9 8 7 6 5 4 3 2 1

Contents

Chapter 4: What Should Be the Role of the Media in the Legal System?

Why Consider
Opposing Viewpoints?

> *"The only way in which a human being can make some approach to knowing the whole of a subject is by hearing what can be said about it by persons of every variety of opinion and studying all modes in which it can be looked at by every character of mind. No wise man ever acquired his wisdom in any mode but this."*
>
> *John Stuart Mill*

In our media-intensive culture it is not difficult to find differing opinions. Thousands of newspapers and magazines and dozens of radio and television talk shows resound with differing points of view. The difficulty lies in deciding which opinion to agree with and which "experts" seem the most credible. The more inundated we become with differing opinions and claims, the more essential it is to hone critical reading and thinking skills to evaluate these ideas. Opposing Viewpoints books address this problem directly by presenting stimulating debates that can be used to enhance and teach these skills. The varied opinions contained in each book examine many different aspects of a single issue. While examining these conveniently edited opposing views, readers can develop critical thinking skills such as the ability to compare and contrast authors' credibility, facts, argumentation styles, use of persuasive techniques, and other stylistic tools. In short, the Opposing Viewpoints series is an ideal way to attain the higher-level thinking and reading skills so essential in a culture of diverse and contradictory opinions.

In addition to providing a tool for critical thinking, Opposing Viewpoints books challenge readers to question their own strongly held opinions and assumptions. Most people form their opinions on the basis of upbringing, peer pressure, and personal, cultural, or professional bias. By reading carefully balanced opposing views, readers must directly confront new ideas as well as the opinions of those with whom they disagree. This is not to simplistically argue that everyone who reads opposing views will—or should—change his or her opinion. Instead, the series enhances readers' understanding of their own views by encouraging confrontation with opposing ideas. Careful examination of others' views can lead to the readers' understanding of the logical inconsistencies in their own opinions, perspective on why they hold an opinion, and the consideration of the possibility that their opinion requires further evaluation.

Evaluating Other Opinions

To ensure that this type of examination occurs, Opposing Viewpoints books present all types of opinions. Prominent spokespeople on different sides of each issue as well as well-known professionals from many disciplines challenge the reader. An additional goal of the series is to provide a forum for other, less known, or even unpopular viewpoints. The opinion of an ordinary person who has had to make the decision to cut off life support from a terminally ill relative, for example, may be just as valuable and provide just as much insight as a medical ethicist's professional opinion. The editors have two additional purposes in including these less known views. One, the editors encourage readers to respect others' opinions—even when not enhanced by professional credibility. It is only by reading or listening to and objectively evaluating others' ideas that one can determine whether they are worthy of consideration. Two, the inclusion of such viewpoints encourages the important critical thinking skill of objectively evaluating an author's credentials and bias. This evaluation will illuminate an author's reasons for taking a particular stance on an issue and will aid in readers' evaluation of the author's ideas.

It is our hope that these books will give readers a deeper understanding of the issues debated and an appreciation of the complexity of even seemingly simple issues when good and honest people disagree. This awareness is particularly important in a democratic society such as ours in which people enter into public debate to determine the common good. Those with whom one disagrees should not be regarded as enemies but rather as people whose views deserve careful examination and may shed light on one's own.

Thomas Jefferson once said that "difference of opinion leads to inquiry, and inquiry to truth." Jefferson, a broadly educated man, argued that "if a nation expects to be ignorant and free . . . it expects what never was and never will be." As individuals and as a nation, it is imperative that we consider the opinions of others and examine them with skill and discernment. The Opposing Viewpoints series is intended to help readers achieve this goal.

David L. Bender and Bruno Leone,
Founders

"The legal system of the United States reflects the fundamental principle that the
law is the creation of the people and designed to shield citizens from both tyranny and lawlessness, to protect freedom, and to enable society to conduct its
affairs for the welfare of all."

—U.S. Department of State

"It is terrifically important that Americans realize that the founding fathers
created a separation of powers and that
it is not just a lot of congressional interference with a wartime president, but an
essential part of the functioning of our
government that each branch, each
branch has its relative strengths and role,
and that for one branch to over dominate, to over control the other two is not
healthy for the society."

—Tom Foley,
Democratic Speaker of the U.S. House
of Representatives, 1989–1995

Introduction

The legal system in the United States has survived many
challenges since the Constitution was ratified in 1788 as
the supreme law of the land. The Constitution provided for a
system of shared power between three branches of government, the executive, judicial, and legislative. Federal government has specific, enumerated powers, and each of the fifty
sovereign states retains substantial legal authority not granted
to the federal government. As a federalist system, each level of

government has authority to legislate, interpret, and enforce law. Government at each level—local, state, and federal—adheres, in theory, to the principle of separation of powers. A system of checks and balances is intended to ensure that the executive, legislative, or judicial branch will not accumulate excessive powers.

Since the September 11, 2001, attack on the United States, Congress has enacted many controversial laws, and through the executive branch, numerous presidential directives and signing statements have been issued that have dramatically changed the face of the U.S. legal system. Some argue that constitutionally guaranteed protections and checks on excessive executive authority have been compromised in the name of national security. Others contend that, in a time of war, essential powers must be exercised expeditiously, without undue interference with the operational authority of the president and his military commanders. Still others wonder if the so-called War on Terror can be equated with other wars, for example, World War II.

President George W. Bush has asserted that as commander in chief he is constitutionally empowered with "inherent" authority to suspend laws in wartime. This assertion of executive power has drawn some fire from Congress. According to Vermont senator Patrick Leahy "When a White House acts as if it alone knows best, thwarting the accountability of checks and balances, it makes bad decisions, even worse." Former Vice President Al Gore argues, "It is the pitiful state of our legislative branch which primarily explains the failure of our vaunted checks and balances to prevent the dangerous overreach by our Executive Branch which now threatens a radical transformation of the American system."

By contrast, *Washington Times* columnist Alan Nathan asserts, "Once the president is armed with a war resolution, Congress and the judiciary have no more right to micromanage the commander-in-chief than does the president or Congress to overrule a Supreme Court justice following their respective nomination and confirmation of him to the bench. Congress's legitimate right to oversight does not a subordination of the commander-in-chief make."

The president as chief executive has the power to issue executive orders in the form of presidential directives, may veto legislation presented by Congress, or issue signing statements at the time legislation is signed into law. The president is commander in chief of the military and is empowered to appoint judges and other officials. Through the Department of Justice and other executive agencies, the president has the responsibility to ensure that all laws are carried out, and he also retains the power to pardon those convicted of a crime.

Throughout U.S. history there has been a healthy tension between the three interdependent branches of government. But as legal scholars debate the legitimate limits on executive power, and the wisdom and scope of the expansion of these powers during times of war, citizens who are educated about the constitutional principles and democratic ideals that have shaped the U.S. legal system must be a vital element in the discussion.

William Kristol and Gary Schmitt, writing in the *Washington Post*, contend that "the issue of executive power and the law in our constitutional order is more complicated than the current debate would suggest. It is not easy to answer the question whether the president, acting in this gray area, is 'breaking the law.' It is not easy because the Founders intended the executive to have—believed the executive needed to have—some powers in the national security area that were extralegal but constitutional."

Commentator Glenn Greenwald states: "The notion that the president can act without limitations from the other two branches of government is supported by neither express constitutional provisions nor this country's basic founding principles. Indeed, the unrestrained and unchecked executive branch . . . is precisely what the founders sought to avoid when they created a system of government with three co-equal branches, designed to share power in every area, including—perhaps especially—in matters of war."

The debate about separation of powers in the U.S. legal system has been heated and ongoing and will likely continue, with the outcome of the struggle between the interdependent branches of government affecting the operation and integrity of the U.S. legal system for generations to come.

In *Opposing Viewpoints: Legal System*, many controversial aspects of the U.S. legal system are presented for examination. Its chapters explore various factors associated with the legal system and how they are interpreted. The authors present differing viewpoints on how the legal system functions and how well and how fairly it serves the people of the United States, particularly in times of international conflict when national security is one issue facing each branch of government and when constitutionally provided checks on excessive power are particularly important.

OPPOSING
VIEWPOINTS®
SERIES

CHAPTER 1

Is the U.S. Legal System in Jeopardy?

Chapter Preface

One of the more hotly debated laws enacted during the tenure of President George W. Bush is the controversial USA PATRIOT Act. This bill, officially known as the "Uniting and Strengthening America by Providing Appropriate Tools Required to Intercept and Obstruct Terrorism Act of 2001," was passed with scant congressional oversight and debate just two weeks after the attacks on the World Trade Center in New York City and the Pentagon in Washington, D.C. The "USA PATRIOT Improvement and Reauthorization Act of 2005," was intended to "extend and modify authorities needed to combat terrorism, and for other purposes." President Bush issued a signing statement indicating that he would interpret certain sections of the 2005 law—those mandating disclosure of information to congressional oversight committees—"in a manner consistent with the president's constitutional authority to supervise the unitary executive branch and to withhold information the disclosure of which could impair foreign relations, national security, the deliberative processes of the Executive, or the performance of the Executive's constitutional duties".

During the course of his tenure as chief executive, George W. Bush has issued more than one hundred presidential signing statements indicating his intent to interpret or restrict congressional legislation. In 2007, a Government Accountability Office (GAO) report commissioned by Democratic Senator Robert Byrd of West Virginia, and Representative John Conyers, a Democrat from Michigan, surveyed the effect of presidential signing statements issued on eleven of the twelve congressional spending bills in 2006. The signing statements singled out 160 specific provisions in those bills. The GAO concluded that the statements have effectively nullified the law in about 30 percent of the audited legislation, including spending bills for the war in Iraq.

Many critics of such presidential signing statements, such as Democratic Senator Dianne Feinstein, as reported in May 2006 in the *San Francisco Chronicle*, have accused President Bush of abusing his authority. "The president is usurping power from both the legislative and the judicial branches and destroying this balance that has served our country so well," she argues.

Supporters of the president's authority, however, contend that the president, in his role as commander in chief, has the right to control employees and officers of the executive branch and to withhold information from Congress for national security reasons. "Congress is too large and unwieldy to take the swift and decisive action required in wartime," argues former Justice Department attorney John Yoo, professor of law at the University of California, Berkeley. "Even when it has access to the same intelligence as the executive branch, as with Iraq, Congress's loose, decentralized structure would paralyze American policy while foreign threats grow."

The USA PATRIOT Act expanded the use of National Security Letters (NSLs) authorizing agents to seize telephone, business, and financial records without prior judicial approval. In a 2007 Justice Department investigation of the Federal Bureau of Investigation's (FBI) use of National Security Letters, Inspector General Glenn A. Fine found that of the more than 56,000 NSL requests made each year since the Patriot Act was enacted, many were issued without proper authority, cited incorrect statutes, or sought information they were not legally authorized to obtain.

Despite the "deficiencies in our process," FBI director Robert S. Mueller III contends that national security letters "remain an indispensable investigative tool. NSLs contribute significantly to the FBI's ability to carry out its national security responsibilities by directly supporting its counterterrorism, counterintelligence, and intelligence missions. NSLs also allow the FBI to obtain information to eliminate concerns about individuals and close down investigations with a high degree of confidence that there is no terrorism or adverse intelligence-gathering threat."

By contrast, Caroline Fredrickson, director of the ACLU Washington Legislative Office states: "The Patriot Act's expansion of the NSL power was fatally flawed from the beginning because there is no judicial review. Although the NSL process is inadequate, the FBI flouted even those weak rules, because there is no scrutiny and no accountability. No one is above the law, neither the FBI nor the attorney general, and Congress needs to hold them accountable and prevent future violations by fixing the Patriot Act."

In chapter 1, various authors present their views on the state of the U.S. legal system and the effect of laws such as the USA PATRIOT Act and the Military Commissions Act, as well as the chief executive's use of presidential signing statements. These issues are at the center of the debate on the integrity of the U.S. legal system.

"[The USA PATRIOT Act] will improve our nation's security while we safeguard the civil liberties of our people. The legislation strengthens the Justice Department so it can better detect and disrupt terrorist threats. And the bill gives law enforcement new tools to combat threats to our citizens from international terrorists to local drug dealers."

The USA PATRIOT Act Strengthens the Legal System

George W. Bush

George W. Bush, the forty-third president of the United States, was sworn in for a second term on January 20, 2005. The following viewpoint is from President Bush's remarks as he signed into law the "USA PATRIOT Improvement and Reauthorization Act." The president contends that the wars in Afghanistan and Iraq have "brought down two regimes that supported terrorism." He argues that the USA PATRIOT Act is needed to improve security and to provide the necessary legal tools to go after terrorists in the United States.

George W. Bush, "President Signs USA PATRIOT Improvement and Reauthorization Act," Office of the Press Secretary, The White House, March 9, 2006, www.whitehouse .gov.

As you read, consider the following questions:

1. President Bush contends that the USA PATRIOT Act has strengthened national security. In the president's view, in what ways does the law accomplish this?
2. What new government position was created by passage of the USA PATRIOT Act?
3. How does the USA PATRIOT Act address the illegal manufacture of methamphetamine?

The USA PATRIOT Improvement and Reauthorization Act is a really important piece of legislation. It is a piece of legislation that's vital to win the war on terror and to protect the American people.

The law allows our intelligence and law enforcement officials to continue to share information. It allows them to continue to use tools against terrorists that they used against—that they use against drug dealers and other criminals. [The USA PATRIOT Act] will improve our nation's security while we safeguard the civil liberties of our people. The legislation strengthens the Justice Department so it can better detect and disrupt terrorist threats. And the bill gives law enforcement new tools to combat threats to our citizens from international terrorists to local drug dealers.

America remains a nation at war. The war reached our shores on September the 11th, 2001. On that morning, we saw clearly the violence and hatred of a new enemy. We saw the terrorists' destructive vision for us when they killed nearly 3,000 men, women, and children.

In the face of this ruthless threat, our nation has made a clear choice: We will confront this mortal danger, we will stay on the offensive, and we're not going to wait to be attacked again. Since September the 11th, 2001, we have taken the fight to the enemy. We've hunted terrorists in the mountains of Afghanistan, cities of Iraq, the islands of Southeast Asia, and everywhere else they plot, plan, and train. Our men and women in uniform have brought down two regimes that supported terrorism. We liberated 50 million people. We've gained new allies in the war on terror.

Fighting Terrorists at Home

As we wage the war on terror overseas, we're also going after the terrorists here at home, and one of the most important tools we have used to protect the American people is the Patriot Act. The Patriot Act closed dangerous gaps in America's law enforcement and intelligence capabilities, gaps the terrorists exploited when they attacked us on September the 11th.

The Patriot Act was passed with overwhelming bipartisan support. It strengthened our national security in two important ways: First, it authorized law enforcement and intelligence officers to share vital information. Before the Patriot Act, criminal investigators were often separated from intelligence officers by a legal and bureaucratic wall. The Patriot Act tore down the wall. And as a result, law enforcement and intelligence officers are sharing information, working together, and bringing terrorists to justice.

Secondly, the Patriot Act has allowed agents to pursue terrorists with the same tools they use against other criminals. Before the Patriot Act, it was easier to track the phone contacts of a drug dealer than the phone contacts of an enemy operative. Before the Patriot Act, it was easier to get the credit card receipts of a tax cheater than trace the financial support of an al Qaeda fundraiser. The Patriot Act corrected these double standards, and the United States is safer as a result.

Over the past four years, America's law enforcement and intelligence personnel have proved the Patriot Act works. Federal, state, and local law enforcement have used the Patriot Act to break up terror cells in Ohio, New York, Oregon and Virginia. We've prosecuted terrorist operatives and supporters in California and Texas, New Jersey, Illinois, Washington, and North Carolina.

Use All Reasonable Means

Why should we allow enemies to annihilate us simply because we lack the clarity or resolve to strike a reasonable balance between a healthy skepticism of government power and the need to take proactive measures to protect ourselves from such threats? The mantra of civil-liberties hard-liners is to "question authority"—even when it is coming to our rescue—then blame that same authority when, hamstrung by civil liberties laws, it fails to save us. The old laws that would prevent FBI agents from stopping the next al-Mihdhar and al-Hazmi were built on the bedrock of a 35-year history of dark, defeating mistrust. More Americans should not die because the peace-at-any-cost fringe and antigovernment paranoids still fighting the ghost of Nixon hate George Bush more than they fear al Qaeda. Ask the American people what they want. They will say that they want the commander in chief to use all reasonable means to catch the people who are trying to rain terror on our cities. Those who cite the soaring principle of individual liberty do not appear to appreciate that our enemies are not seeking to destroy individuals, but whole populations.

Debra Burlingame, "Our Right to Security:
AL Qaeda, not the FBI, Is the Greater Threat to America."
WSJ.com Opinion Journal. *January 30, 2006.*

The Patriot Act has accomplished exactly what it was designed to do. It has helped us detect terror cells, disrupt terrorist plots and save American lives. The bill I sign today extends these vital provisions. It also gives our nation new protections and added defenses.

Added Protections

This legislation creates a new position of Assistant Attorney General for National Security. This will allow the Justice Department to bring together its national security, counterterrorism, counterintelligence and foreign intelligence surveillance operations under a single authority. This reorganization fulfills one of the critical recommendations of the WMD Commission: It will help our brave men and women in law enforcement connect the dots before the terrorists strike.

This bill also will help protect Americans from the growing threat of methamphetamine. Meth is easy to make. It is highly addictive. It is ruining too many lives across our country. The bill introduces common-sense safeguards that would make many of the ingredients used in manufacturing meth harder to obtain in bulk, and easier for law enforcement to track.

For example, the bill places limits on large-scale purchases of over-the-counter drugs that are used to manufacture meth. It requires stores to keep these ingredients behind the counter or in locked display cases. The bill also increases penalties for smuggling and selling of meth. Our nation is committed to protecting our citizens and our young people from the scourge of methamphetamine.

The Patriot Act has served America well, yet we cannot let the fact that America has not been attacked since September the 11th lull us into the illusion that the terrorist threat has disappeared. We still face dangerous enemies. The terrorists haven't lost the will or the ability to kill innocent folks. Our military, law enforcement, homeland security and intelligence professionals are working day and night to protect us from this threat. We're safer for their efforts, and we'll continue to give them the tools to get the job done.

> *"Reauthorization does not make the Patriot Act constitutional. . . . It's clear that some sections of the Patriot Act went too far, too fast and violate the fundamental freedoms of Americans."*

The USA PATRIOT Act Undermines the Legal System

American Civil Liberties Union

The American Civil Liberties Union, founded in 1920, is a membership organization that works in courts, legislatures, and communities to defend and preserve the individual rights and liberties guaranteed by the U.S. Constitution and laws of the United States. The ACLU contends that the USA PATRIOT Act, passed by the U.S. Congress in response to the Sept. 11, 2001, terrorist attacks, has vastly expanded the government's authority to spy on its citizens, while reducing checks and balances on those powers.

As you read, consider the following questions:

1. When the USA PATRIOT Act was first voted on in the U.S. Senate, how many senators opposed the bill? During the reauthorization vote of 2005, by how much had the opposition increased?

American Civil Liberties Union, "The Patriot Act: Where It Stands," March 20, 2007. Copyright © 2007 ACLU, 125 Broad Street, 18th Floor, New York, NY 10004. Reproduced by permission. http://action.aclu.org.

2. According to the ACLU position, which constitutional amendment is violated by warrantless eavesdropping on Americans by the National Security Agency?

3. In the 2006 law reauthorizing the Patriot Act, what is the most serious flaw, in the opinion of the ACLU? What is meant by the "sunset provision"?

The fight to reform the Patriot Act is far from over. Congress failed to include commonsense reforms to the Patriot Act that would target our precious anti-terrorism resources on suspected foreign terrorists rather than invading the privacy of innocent people through fishing expeditions into their financial, medical, library and Internet records.

The ACLU is disappointed and deeply concerned with Congress' capitulation to the White House's opposition to modest but meaningful changes that would better protect the privacy and civil liberties of all American residents. . . .

The Patriot Act debate has come a long way in the last four years. When the Senate first voted on the Patriot Act, only one Senator opposed it—on [the 2006] reauthorization vote, that number increased ten-fold. And a bipartisan group of 52 Senators stood up to the administration and filibustered the reauthorization bill.

In the House, bipartisan majorities supported bills to limit the reach of the Patriot Act by placing better checks and balances into the law—moves that were ultimately overridden by the Republican House leadership at the behest of the Bush administration's knee-jerk opposition to common-sense reforms. . . .

The Patriot Act Debate Is Far from Over

The ACLU will continue to press for meaningful reforms. Along with our bipartisan allies, the ACLU will continue to push for common-sense changes to be made to the Patriot Act to bring it in line with the Constitution by restoring much needed checks and balances.

More than 400 communities across the nation have passed resolutions seeking reforms of the Patriot Act. These communities range from the conservative state of Montana to the progressive state of Hawaii; and from cities as large as New York to small towns like Elko, Nevada. Unfortunately, due to pressure from the White House, Congress did not listen to the people.

Reauthorization does not make the Patriot Act constitutional. It's clear that some sections of the Patriot Act went too far, too fast and violate the fundamental freedoms of Americans.

Fortunately, Congress did reject efforts, supported by administration allies, to expand the Patriot Act to further encroach on constitutional liberties. Lawmakers flatly rejected the "Domestic Security Enhancement Act," the so-called "Patriot Act 2." Congress also refused to act on the completely unwarranted proposal by the administration to allow the FBI to subpoena "any tangible thing" without court approval in intelligence investigations.

The Patriot Act debate has been about preserving fundamental American values. Unfortunately, despite all of the changes the Patriot Act made to the Foreign Intelligence Surveillance Act (FISA) back in 2001, President Bush has arrogated to himself the unconstitutional . . . power to ignore FISA's requirement of judicial oversight over all wiretapping of U.S. persons. Even if we were to win all of the reforms needed to fix the Patriot Act until Americans demand that the president be required to follow the law any such changes could be ignored under the current regime.

President Bush's instigation of warrantless eavesdropping on Americans by the National Security Agency violates the Americans' Fourth Amendment rights and demonstrates a total disregard for the rule of law. Our system of government requires that the power of any president must not be unchecked—Americans demand a strong system of checks and balances. Presidents must faithfully execute the laws passed by Congress and cannot simply ignore those laws.

This administration has taken an extreme view on executive power. Congress must restore the rule of law and insist that Americans' rights be protected. Our great nation can, and must, be both safe and free.

Patriot Act Reauthorization

The reauthorization bill that became law in 2006 retains the most serious flaws from the original Patriot Act, primarily failing to require that any private records sought in an intelligence investigation be about suspected foreign terrorists or Americans conspiring with them.

Congress passed the Patriot Act, with very little debate, just 45 days after 9/11, when emotions ran high and lawmakers were under pressure to do something, pass anything, in response. Some Members of Congress had less than an hour to read the extensive changes in the law before voting.

Many Members of Congress, worried about the potential for abuse, demanded that the government include "sunsets" on some of the most extreme parts of the act. Under the sunset provision, these powers were to be reconsidered by Congress or they were to expire.

Partisans tried to rush through the reauthorization process at the beginning of 2005, at the administration's request that all the powers be made permanent with no changes. While multiple hearings were held in both the House and Senate on the Patriot Act itself, neither chamber held hearings on the actual changes to the law that were proposed. And, the House leadership refused to allow key reforms to the final bill to get an up or down vote by the full House. In the Senate, partisan leadership similarly blocked efforts to get up or down votes

"Ideology of Lawlessness"

One of the very few attempts over the last six years from Congress to impose at least some safeguards on the use of radical new executive powers was to require that the FBI report to Congress on the issuance of National Security Letters (NSLs) so that Congress could at least know about (and, theoretically, take action in response to) any abuse of these powers. But the minute George Bush got what he wanted—re-authorization of the Patriot Act—he proclaimed for all the world to hear that he had the power to violate those provisions and refuse to comply with such safeguards. And now it is revealed that the FBI has, in fact, violated the very provisions which the President proclaimed he could violate. . . .

The Bush administration has created vast and *permanent* databases to collect and store evidence revealing the private activities of millions of . . . American citizens. When the FBI obtains information essentially in secret—with no judicial oversight—that information is stored in those databases. This is all being done by the executive branch with no safeguards and no oversight . . .

The story here is not merely that the FBI is breaking the law and abusing these powers. . . . The story is that the FBI is ignoring the very legal obligations which George Bush vowed were not obligations at all, but mere suggestions to be accepted only if he willed it. It is yet another vivid example proving that the President's ideology of lawlessness exists not merely in theory, but as the governing doctrine under which the executive branch has acted, time and again and as deliberately as possible, in violation of whatever laws it deems inconvenient.

Glenn Greenwald, "The FBI's lawbreaking is tied directly to President Bush," salon.com, March 9, 2007. www.salon.com.

on key amendments to reform the Patriot Act. Clearly, congressional leaders feared that if lawmakers were allowed a fair vote on the most needed reforms that they would pass.

The efforts to make almost all of the Patriot Act permanent with few substantive reforms was met by strong resistance from an unlikely chorus across the political spectrum. The ACLU worked with organizations on the left and the right to press for reforms, such as Patriots to Restore Checks and Balances, a coalition including such conservative organizations like the American Conservative Union and Americans for Tax Reform to call for meaningful changes.

The House and Senate passed different versions of legislation to reauthorize the Patriot Act. Since they were not the same bill, the differences were resolved in a "conference committee" with representatives from both chambers, but critical compromises were made while excluding Democrats from negotiations. The ensuing conference report failed to include the most important civil liberties protections included in the Senate version of the bill. A final bill and a small amendments package have now passed both houses of Congress. The amended Patriot Act continues to fail to adequately protect the privacy rights of innocent, ordinary people in this country.

> "The military commissions authorized by this legislation are lawful, fair and necessary. With the Military Commissions Act, the legislative and executive branches have agreed on a system that meets our national security needs."

The Military Commissions Act of 2006 Protects National Security

Office of the Press Secretary, The White House

The White House press secretary for President George W. Bush released a fact sheet on the Military Commissions Act of 2006 on October 17, 2006, to explain to American citizens how the Act will preserve the tools needed to help save American lives in an age of terrorist threats. A key provision of the Act will permit the Central Intelligence Agency to continue its program for questioning key terrorist leaders and operatives. This provision was identified by the Bush administration as being necessary for saving American lives.

Office of the Press Secretary, The White House, "Fact Sheet: The Military Commissions Act of 2006," October 17, 2006. www.whitehouse.gov.

As you read, consider the following:

1. The Bush administration asserts that the Military Commissions Act will allow for "full and fair trials." What specific groups of detainees did the lawmakers intend to prosecute?

2. Why would the law spell out specific and recognizable offenses as guidelines to use when questioning terrorists? How might this help the military personnel charged with interrogation?

3. Information gained from questioning terrorists in CIA custody has protected the American homeland from attack, according to the Bush administration. In what specific incidents has this been accomplished?

The Military Commissions Act Of 2006, will preserve the tools needed to help save American lives. This bill will allow the CIA to continue its program for questioning key terrorist leaders and operatives like Khalid Sheikh Mohammed— the man believed to be the mastermind of the 9/11 attacks. This program has been one of the most successful intelligence efforts in American history, and the Military Commissions Act will ensure that we can continue using this vital tool to protect the American people for years to come. With this bill, America reaffirms our determination to win the War on Terror.

The Military Commissions Act will also allow us to prosecute captured terrorists for war crimes through full and fair trials. With this legislation, those believed to have orchestrated the murder of nearly 3,000 innocent people on 9/11 will face justice. We will also seek to prosecute those believed to be responsible for the attack on the USS Cole and an operative believed to have been involved in the bombings of the American embassies in Kenya and Tanzania.

The Military Commissions Act Will Allow the CIA to Continue Its Program for Questioning Terrorists

When the president proposed this legislation, he explained that his one test for the bill Congress produced would be whether it would allow the CIA program to continue—and this bill meets that test. It allows for the clarity our intelligence professionals need to continue questioning terrorists and saving lives. This bill:

- Provides legal protections that ensure our military and intelligence personnel will not have to fear lawsuits filed by terrorists simply for doing their jobs;

- Spells out specific, recognizable offenses that would be considered crimes in the handling of detainees—so that our men and women who question captured terrorists can perform their duties to the fullest extent of the law; and

- Complies with both the spirit and the letter of our international obligations.

Were it not for the CIA program, our intelligence community believes al-Qaeda and its allies would have succeeded in attacking the American homeland again. Information from terrorists in CIA custody has played a role in the capture or questioning of nearly every senior al-Qaeda member or associate detained by the United States and its allies since this program began. The CIA program helped us:

- Gain vital intelligence from Khalid Sheikh Mohammed and Ramzi bin al Shibh—two of the men believed to have helped plan and facilitate the 9/11 attacks;

Military Commission Act Upholds Key Tool in War on Terror

"[The U.S. Court of Appeals' February 2007] decision was the correct one. It upholds a key tool in the war on terror, the Military Commissions Act of 2006, and it addresses the flawed constitutional arguments by critics of this legislation who have engaged in a campaign of misinformation regarding America's treatment of captured enemy combatants. The detainees held at Guantanamo Bay do not have an unfettered constitutional right to file habeas corpus petitions in U.S. federal courts. The United States has never allowed such access to its court system by foreign enemies captured on the battlefield.

"Congress has twice spoken to remove this unprecedented and burdensome litigation from the federal courts. We expect the courts to respect the will of Congress.

"While habeas review is not permitted, Guantanamo detainees do receive a fair and manageable appeals process, including their day in federal court. Importantly, even without habeas review, these unlawful combatants receive more due process rights than are required for prisoners of war under the Geneva Convention. This is entirely consistent with America's values and our Constitution.

"In fact, the legal and humane actions of the U.S. government stand in stark contrast to our al-Qaeda enemies who behead those they capture."

Senator John Cornyn,
"Military Commission Act Decision Upholds Key Tool
in War on Terror," February 20, 2007. http://cornyn.senate.gov.

- Break up a cell of 17 Southeast Asian terrorist operatives being groomed for attacks inside the United States;

- Uncover key operatives in al-Qaeda's biological weapons program—including a cell developing anthrax to be used in terrorist attacks;

- Identify terrorists who were sent to case targets inside the United States, including financial buildings in major cities along the East Coast; and

- Stop a planned strike on U.S. Marines in Djibouti, a planned attack on the U.S. Consulate in Karachi, and a plot to hijack passenger planes and fly them into Heathrow Airport and Canary Wharf in London.

The Military Commissions Authorized by This Legislation Are Lawful, Fair, and Necessary

With The Military Commissions Act, the legislative and executive branches have agreed on a system that meets our national security needs. In the months after 9/11, the President authorized a system of military commissions to try foreign terrorists accused of war crimes. These commissions were similar to those used for trying enemy combatants in the Revolutionary War, the Civil War, and World War II. After the legality of this system was challenged and the Supreme Court ruled that military commissions need explicit authorization by Congress, the President asked Congress for that authority—and Congress provided it.

> *"The Military Commissions Act is emblematic of many of the abuses of government power that have shamed our country: extraordinary rendition, torture, indefinite imprisonment without charge or access to a lawyer, and illegal eavesdropping on our telephone calls and emails."*

The Military Commissions Act of 2006 Infringes on Judicial Due Process

Anthony D. Romero

Anthony D. Romero is the executive director of the American Civil Liberties Union. The ACLU's top legislative priority is turning back the Military Commissions Act of 2006, a law that the ACLU considers to be "ill-conceived, extremely harmful and un-American." In this viewpoint, Romero details the ordeal of ACLU client Khaled el-Masri, a German citizen abducted in Macedonia and turned over to the CIA. The el-Masri case, Romero contends, illustrates how the Military Commissions Act has "ignored the Constitution and undercut America's commitment to the rule of law."

Anthony D. Romero, "The New Congress and Restoring a Cornerstone of Our Constitution," *Civil Liberties,*, Winter 2007, pp. 9–11. Reproduced by permission.

As you read, consider the following questions:

1. How does Romero define the term "extraordinary rendition?"
2. Under the provisions of the Military Commissions Act of 2006, who has authority to declare a person an "enemy combatant"? How long can a person so accused be held?
3. What does the right of *habeus corpus* mean?

The outrages of the Bush administration have been many and the abuses of power are stacked high. America's voters have now spoken and we will soon have a new Congress—one that offers the promise of belatedly restoring a check on a president who needed a reminder that he is not a "hereditary king."

It is imperative that the new Congress act quickly to pull back a law—the Military Commissions Act—that among other problems removed a cornerstone of both our Constitution and our country's legal heritage: *habeus corpus*.

Habeus corpus—Latin for "you have the body"—is the legal instrument or "writ" via which a detained individual can seek release from unlawful imprisonment. It has been part of Western law for 800 years and was incorporated into our Consitution when our Founders enshrined it in Article One. This "Great Writ" is the foundation of our nation's limits on executive power, intended to protect due process and prevent indefinite detention without judicial review.

Congress approved, and the president signed, the Military Commissions Act just weeks before the Nov. 7 [2006] elections. This Act undermines both our Constitution and the rule of law.

The Military Commissions Act is emblematic of many of the abuses of government power that have shamed our country: extraordinary rendition, torture, indefinite imprisonment without charge or access to a lawyer, and illegal eavesdropping on our telephone calls and emails.

For instance, take the government's once-secret program of extraordinary rendition—in which individuals are kidnapped by our government and whisked away to foreign countries to be held indefinitely in secret, government-funded torture cells. This nightmarish ordeal is precisely what happened to ACLU client Khaled el-Masri. Abducted in Macedonia and turned over to the CIA, this innocent German citizen was held for 23 days before being severely beaten, drugged. and flown to Afghanistan on an airplane leased by U.S. government agents. There, he was tortured and detained in the notorious "Salt Pit" prison—even after our government realized that this was a case of mistaken identity. Five months after being kidnapped, Mr. el-Masri was led out of his cell, blindfolded, handcuffed, chained to the seat of a plane, flown to Albania and—without explanation—abandoned on a hillside at night. The ACLU represents him in a federal lawsuit, arguing that his human rights and constitutional rights were taken from him by the U.S. government. We also brought Mr. el-Masri to the United States for meetings with the press and Congress to draw greater attention to the issues of kidnapping and torture and other violations of human rights.

The President first denied that rendition and these torture prisons existed at all. When that lie was exposed, he reversed course and transferred more than a dozen detainees from the secret detention camps to a well-known detention camp— Guantánamo Bay Naval Base—where they joined hundreds of other detainees, some of whom have been held for nearly five years with no access to courts, no meaningful contact with their families and no prospect of a fair trial.

Under the terms of the Military Commissions Act, any non-U.S. citizen or resident who—correctly or incorrectly— the President declares is an "enemy combatant" is treated this way:

- They lose *habeas*, the right to seek release from unlawful imprisonment.

- They lose the right to due process under the law.

- They lose the right to be told why they have been imprisoned or even what they are accused of having done.

- They may be convicted on the basis of evidence that was beaten out of a witness.

- These people can be locked up forever, out of sight, out of communication, left to rot in modern-day detention camps.

By enacting this shameful law, our government has ignored the Constitution and undercut America's commitment to the rule of law. When our government does not follow the law, it threatens all of our freedoms and undermines what it means be an American.

There are some reasons to believe this law can be reversed. Here is what Senator Patrick Leahy (D-VT)—the next chairman of the Senate Judiciary Committee—had to say in late September when he announced he would be voting against the Military Commissions Act:

"Passing laws that remove the few checks against mistreatment of prisoners will not help us win the battle for the hearts and minds of the generation of young people around the world being recruited by Osama bin Laden and al Qaeda. Authorizing indefinite detention of anybody the government designates—without any proceedings and without any recourse—is what our worst critics claim the United States would do, not what American values, traditions and our rule of law would have us do."

Senator Gordon Smith (R-OR) also spoke out against the bill:

"A responsibility this nation has always assumed is to ensure that no one is held prisoner unjustly. Stripping courts of their authority to hear habeas claims is a frontal attack on our judiciary and its institutions, as well as our civil rights laws. Habeas corpus is a cornerstone of our consitutional order, and a suspension of that right, whether for U.S. citizens or foreigners under U.S. control, ought to trouble us all. The right to judicial appeal is enshrined in our Constitution. It is part and parcel of the rule of law. The Supreme Court has described the writ of habeas corpus as 'the fundamental instrument for safeguarding individual freedom agaisnt arbitrary and lawless State action.'"

And here are the comments of Senator Christopher Dodd (D-CT) in his October speech to the Council on Foreign Relations:

"One action we can take is to re-think our treatment of enemy combatants—because the manner in which we treat those whom we most despise or distrust is what distinguishes us as a nation."

Separately, Senators Leahy, Smith, and Dodd all made the point that in the aftermath of World War II, the United States had to decide how to deal with Hitler's Nazi war criminals and their unimaginably horrific crimes against humanity. Senator Dodd's comments about the context of that decision are representative:

"Why not just shoot the guilty, as Winston Churchill wanted to do? Why not just give in to vengeance, which was certainly within our ability—and, many argued, within our right?

"Ultimately, we chose a different course. We decided that, if the judgments rendered at Nuremberg were to truly reflect the Allies' commitment to defeating tyranny and lawlessness, those judgments would have to come following a trial. Not a trial in name, but a trial in fact. A trial that gave defendants

Extraordinary Powers

The Military Commissions Act concentrates extraordinary power in the hands of the president, allowing President Bush to identify anyone he chooses, including American citizens, as enemy combatants. As such, they can be imprisoned indefinitely, interrogated by methods approved only by the president, and deprived of any court review for their case. According to this law, any president of the United States will now be able to personally interpret the Geneva Conventions as he or she sees fit, confident that such interpretations must stand inviolate. In effect, the courts will be prevented from hearing any challenge to the president's decisions.

And because the president is, according to the bill, able to "promulgate administrative regulations . . . which are not grave breaches of the Geneva Convention," almost all the acts we saw committed in the photos of Abu Ghraib could be decreed by any president as lawful. . . .

Marianne Partridge, "Legalizing AbuGhraib,"
Santa Barbara Independent, *October 5, 2006.*

certain rights—such as the right to be represented by counsel, to know the charges brought, to present a defense, and to be judged by impartial finders of fact."

And that's exactly the point. When someone is suspected of committing an offense—even the most heinous crime—if we fail to provide even the most basic rights to the accused, we diminish ourselves and our core American values.

These are not new concepts for America. On March 5, 1770—six years before the creation of the United States of America—three Americans were killed and two more were mortally wounded in a hail of gunfire from British troops, in what would later come to be known as the Boston Massacre. Eight soldiers thought responsible for the bloodshed were arrested and put on trial the following fall. Three lawyers served as the British soldiers' defense attorneys, one of whom was a 34-year-old man by the name of John Adams. Twenty-seven years before he would become the second president of the United States, Adams was a staunch advocate of American freedom from British rule; however, he also believed that any person accused of a crime deserved a proper defense.

In the end, six of the eight soldiers were acquitted, while two—the soldiers whom the prosecution had proven clearly fired shots—were convicted of manslaughter. Adams was roundly criticized for his passionate defense of the soldiers and his law practice suffered. Later, however, he would write:

> "The part I took in defense of Cptn. Preston and the Soldiers, procured me anxiety, and obloquy enough. It was, however, one of the most gallant, generous, manly and disinterested actions of my whole life, and one of the best pieces of service I ever rendered my country. Judgement of death against those soldiers would have been as foul a stain upon this country as the executions of the Quakers or Witches, anciently."

More than two centuries later, the Military Commissions Act of 2006 is as foul a stain upon this country as John Adams could have imagined. Turning back this ill-conceived, extremely harmful and un-American law is the ACLU's top legislative priority and we will spare no effort in this fight. The time to restore meaningful congressional oversight of the executive branch is long overdue. We will work to ensure that Congress takes early and decisive action to restore the protections of *habeas* to people who have been designated "enemy combatants," ban the use of coerced evidence in military commissions, limit the President's unfettered authority to define torture and abuse, end government kidnapping and torture, and close Guantánamo. We will lead the effort to revive our nation's commitment to law and freedom. But we weill need your help in this campaign. Now is not the time to let our democracy become a spectator sport.

> *"This practice of issuing signing statements . . . is consistent with, and derives from, the President's constitutional obligations, and is an ordinary part of a respectful constitutional dialogue between the branches."*

Presidential Signing Statements Ensure that New Laws Are Constitutional

Michelle E. Boardman

Michelle E. Boardman is an assistant professor of law at George Mason University. She served as the deputy assistant attorney general in the Office of Legal Counsel, U.S. Department of Justice, when she provided testimony before the U.S. House of Representatives Committee on the Judiciary regarding presidential signing statements. Boardman's testimony was repeated in January 2007, attributed to John P. Elwood, of the U.S. Department of Justice. In this viewpoint, Boardman speaks for the United States Department of Justice and contends that the practice of issuing signing statements is consistent with, and derives from, the

Michelle E. Boardman, "Presidential Signing Statements," testimony before the Committee on the Judiciary, United States Senate, June 27, 2006. http://judiciary.senate.gov. Identical speech delivered January 31, 2007, as "Statement of John P. Elwood, Deputy Assistant Attorney General, Office of Legal Counsel, United States Department of Justice."

president's constitutional obligations. Presidential signing statements, she asserts, help ensure that laws are interpreted and executed in a manner consistent with the Constitution.

As you read, consider the following questions:

1. According to Boardman, what are some reasons to use a presidential signing statement?

2. How does Boardman answer critics' charges that constitutional signing statements are a "power grab"?

3. What three specific constitutional provisions did President Bush seek to preserve with constitutional signing statements, according to Boardman?

Like most Presidents before him, President Bush occasionally issues statements on signing legislation into law. Presidents have used these "signing statements" for a variety of purposes. At times Presidents use signing statements to explain to the public why the President endorses a bill and what the President understands to be its likely effect. At other times, Presidents use the statements to guide subordinate officers within the Executive Branch in enforcing or administering a particular provision.

Presidents throughout history also have issued what may be called "constitutional" signing statements, and it is this use of the signing statement that has recently been the subject of public attention. Presidents are sworn to "preserve, protect, and defend the Constitution," and thus are responsible for ensuring that the manner in which they enforce acts of Congress is consistent with America's founding document. . . .

President Bush, like many of his predecessors dating back to as early as President James Monroe, has issued constitutional signing statements. The constitutional concerns identified in these statements often pertain to provisions of law that could be read to infringe explicit constitutional provisions (such as the Recommendations Clause, the Presentment Clauses, and the Appointments Clause) or to violate specific constitutional holdings of the Supreme Court. As such President Bush's signing statements are indistinguishable from those issued by past Presidents. In addition, the number of such statements issued by President Bush is in keeping with the number issued by every President during the past quarter century.

Essential to Constitutional Dialog

It is important to establish at the outset what presidential signing statements are not: an attempt to "cherry-pick" among the parts of a duly enacted law [parts] that the President will choose to follow, or an attempt unilaterally to redefine what the law is after its enactment. Presidential signing statements are, rather, a statement by the President explaining his interpretation of and responsibilities under the law, and they are therefore an essential part of the constitutional dialogue between the branches that has been a part of the etiquette of government since the early days of the Republic. Nor are signing statements an attempt to "override" duly enacted laws, as some critics have suggested. Many constitutional signing statements are an attempt to preserve the enduring balance between co-equal branches, but this preservation does not mean that the President will not enforce the provision as enacted. . . .

A surprising number of statutes enacted by Congress attempt to require the approval of a congressional committee before execution of a law, despite well-settled Supreme Court precedent that such "legislative veto" provisions violate the Presentment and Bicameralism Clauses of the Constitution. . . .

As long as these provisions are placed in otherwise constitutional bills, signing statements serve the appropriate function of reminding Congress and members of the Executive Branch of their deficiency. Again, however, President Bush and past Presidents to our knowledge have not ignored these provisions, but have instead done their best to apply them in a manner that does not violate the Constitution by ordering Executive Branch officials to notify congressional committees as anticipated by the provisions. In short, where a President has no choice but to avoid a constitutional violation, the President's best course is to announce publicly his intention to construe the provision constitutionally. Where the constitutional violation stems not from the substance of a provision but from its mandatory nature, as with the Appointments Clause, the President's best course is to note the deficiency, leaving the President free to act in accordance with the provision as a matter of policy.

In another category of cases, Presidents recognize a statute as constitutional on its face, and anticipate that it will be applied constitutionally, but also foresee that in extreme or unanticipated circumstances it could raise the possibility of an unconstitutional application. An appropriate signing statement may therefore announce that the President fully intends to apply the law as far as possible, consistent with his duty to the Constitution.

To the charge that constitutional signing statements are a "power grab" and encroach on Congress's power to write the law, these examples reveal two flaws. First, the signing statements do not diminish congressional power, because Congress has no power to enact unconstitutional laws. This fact is true whether the President issues a constitutional signing statement or not. Second, the statements do not augment presidential power. Where Congress, perhaps inadvertently, exceeds its own power in violation of the Constitution, the President is bound to defer to the Constitution. The President cannot adopt the provisions he prefers and ignore those he does not; he must execute the law as the Constitution requires. . . .

This practice of issuing signing statements does not mean that a President has acted contrary to law or the Legislative Branch. The practice is consistent with, and derives from, the

President's constitutional obligations, and is an ordinary part of a respectful constitutional dialogue between the branches. When Congress passes legislation containing provisions that could be construed or applied in certain cases in a manner contrary to well-settled constitutional principles, the President can and should take steps to ensure that such laws are interpreted and executed in a manner consistent with the Constitution. The Supreme Court specifically has stated that the President has the power to "supervise and guide [Executive officers'] construction of the statutes under which they act in order to secure that unitary and uniform execution of the laws which Article II of the Constitution evidently contemplated in vesting general executive power in the President alone."

The President takes an oath to "preserve, protect and defend the Constitution of the United States." The President has the responsibility and duty also to faithfully execute the laws of the United States. But these duties are not in conflict: the law the President must execute includes the Constitution—the supreme law of the land. Because the Constitution is supreme over all other law, the President must resolve any conflict between statutory law and the Constitution in favor of the Constitution, just as courts must.

This presidential responsibility may arise most sharply when the President is charged with executing a statute, passed by a previous Congress and signed by a prior President, a provision of which is he finds unconstitutional under intervening Supreme Court precedent. A President that places the statutory law over the constitutional law in this instance would fail in his duty faithfully to execute the laws. The principle is equally sound where the Supreme Court has yet to rule on an issue, but the President has determined that a statutory law violates the Constitution. To say that the principle is not equally sound in this context is to deny the President's independent responsibility to interpret and uphold the Constitu-

The Power of Presidential Signing Statements

An American Bar Association Task Force issued a head-scratching report in 2006 which concluded that "the issuance of presidential signing statements that claim the authority or state the intention to disregard or decline to enforce all or part of a law the president has signed" is "contrary to the rule of law and our constitutional system of separation of powers." That this conclusion is false is well known to constitutional law scholars and, one assumes, to the current and former law school deans on the task force.

For decades presidents have used signing statements to express constitutional objections to specific provisions in bills that bear their signatures. Signing statements typically argue that although a bill is in the public interest, specific provisions violate the president's commander-in-chief power, his authority over appointments, his control over foreign relations, his supervision of subordinates in the executive branch, or his ability to maintain secrecy for national security. . . .

It is true that Bush has challenged more statutory provisions than his predecessors have, but whether he has been justified in doing so depends on whether his constitutional arguments are valid.

It may be that Bush has simply applied the same theories that other presidents have, but has done so more systematically. It may be that Bush has expanded those theories on the margin but that these expansions are justified under the proper reading of the Constitution or in light of changed circumstances. These are important questions that the Bar Association Task Force has ignored in its eagerness to jump on the antisigning statement bandwagon. . . .

Curtis Bradley and Eric Posner, "Signing Statements:
It's A President's Right," The Boston Globe, August 3, 2006.

tion. It is to leave the defense of the Constitution only to two, not three, of the branches of our government. . . .

Preserving Constitutional Provisions

- Presidents commonly have raised concern when Congress purports to require the President to submit legislative recommendations, because the Constitution vests the President with discretion to do so when he sees fit, stating that he "shall from time to time . . . recommend to [Congress's] Consideration such Measures as he shall judge necessary and expedient.". . .

- Presentment Clauses. Presidents commonly raise concern when Congress purports to authorize a single House of Congress to take action on a matter in violation of the well established rule, embodied in the Supreme Court's decision, that Congress can act only by "passage by a majority of both Houses and presentment to the President.". . .

- Appointments Clause. The Appointments Clause of the Constitution provides that the President, with the advice and consent of the Senate, shall appoint principal officers of the United States (heads of agencies, for example); and that "inferior officers" can be appointed only by the President, by the heads of "Departments" (agencies), or by the courts. Presidents commonly raise a concern when bills seem to restrict the President's ability to appoint officers, or to vest entities other than the President, agency heads, or courts with the power to appoint officers. . . .

- Confidentiality of national security information. The Supreme Court has held that the Constitution gives the President authority to control the access of Executive Branch officials to classified information. The Supreme Court has stated that the President's "authority to classify and control access to information bearing on national security and to determine whether an individual is sufficiently trustworthy to occupy a position in the Executive Branch that will give that person access to such information flows primarily from this constitutional investment of power in the President and exists quite apart from any explicit congressional grant." Presidents commonly have issued signing statements when newly enacted provisions might be construed to involve the disclosure of sensitive information. . . .

• Foreign Affairs and Power as Commander in Chief. President Bush also has used signing statements to safeguard the President's well-established role in the Nation's foreign affairs and the President's wartime powers. . . .

Some have argued that President Bush has increased the use of presidential signing statements, but any such increase must be viewed in light of current events and the legislative response to those events. While President Bush has issued numerous signing statements involving foreign affairs and his power as Commander in Chief, the significance of legislation affecting national security has increased markedly since the September 11th attacks and Congress's authorization of the use of military force against the terrorists who perpetrated those attacks. . . .

(Presidential signing) statements are an established part of the President's responsibility to "take Care that the Laws be faithfully executed." U.S. Const., art. II, § 3. Members of Congress and the President will occasionally disagree on a constitutional question. This disagreement does not relieve the President of the obligation to interpret and uphold the

Constitution, but instead supports the candid public announcement of the President's views.

> *"The President does not have unlimited executive authority, not even as Commander-in-Chief of the military. Our government was purposely created with power split between three branches, not concentrated in one."*

Presidential Signing Statements Violate Constitutional Checks and Balances

Jennifer Van Bergen

Jennifer Van Bergen is an author and journalist who writes frequently on civil liberties, human rights, and international law. She also holds a law degree. Bergen is the author of The Twilight of Democracy: The Bush Plan for America. *In this viewpoint, Van Bergen criticizes President Bush's use of "signing statements" as a means of expanding presidential power to the detriment of the long-standing notion of "judicial supremacy." President Bush's interpretation of his executive powers, Van Bergen contends, "gives him license to overrule and bypass Congress or the courts."*

Jennifer Van Bergen, "The Unitary Executive: Is the Doctrine Behind the Bush Presidency Consistent with a Democratic State?" *Findlaw Legal News and Commentary,* January 9, 2006. Copyright © 2006 Findlaw, a Thomson business. This column originally appeared on Findlaw.com. Reproduced by permission.

As you read, consider the following questions:

1. Van Bergen contends that President Bush has used presidential "signing statements" to expand the power of the executive branch. How often did President Bush use these statements during his first term?

2. What is the "coordinate construction theory"? In Van Bergen's view, how does President Bush interpret this theory?

3. What is the "separation of powers"? Why does Van Bergen consider this important to our legal system?

[P]resident] George W. Bush has used presidential "signing statements"—statements issued by the President upon signing a bill into law—to expand his power. Each of his signing statements says that he will interpret the law in question "in a manner consistent with his constitutional authority to supervise the unitary executive branch."

Presidential signing statements have gotten very little media attention. They are, however, highly important documents that define how the President interprets the laws he signs. Presidents use such statements to protect the prerogative of their office and ensure control over the executive branch functions.

Presidents also—since Reagan—have used such statements to create a kind of alternative legislative history. . . .

The alternative legislative history would, according to Dr. Christopher S. Kelley, professor of political science at the Miami University at Oxford, Ohio, "contain certain policy or principles that the administration had lost in its negotiations" with Congress. . . .

President Bush has used presidential signing statements more than any previous president. From President Monroe's administration (1817–25) to the Carter administration (1977–81), the executive branch issued a total of 75 signing statements to protect presidential prerogatives. From Reagan's administration through Clinton's, the total number of signing statements ever issued, by all presidents, rose to a total 322.

In striking contrast to his predecessors, President Bush issued at least 435 signing statements in his first term alone. And, in these statements and in his executive orders, Bush used the term "unitary executive" 95 times. It is important, therefore, to understand what this doctrine means.

What Does the Administration Mean When It Refers to the "Unitary Executive"?

Dr. Kelley notes that the unitary executive doctrine arose as the result of the twin circumstances of Vietnam and Watergate. Kelley asserts that "the faith and trust placed into the presidency was broken as a result of the lies of Vietnam and Watergate," which resulted in a congressional assault on presidential prerogatives.

For example, consider the Foreign Intelligence Surveillance Act (FISA), which Bush evaded when authorizing the NSA to tap without warrants—even those issued by the FISA court. FISA was enacted alter the fall of Nixon with the precise intention of curbing unchecked executive branch surveillance. (Indeed, Nixon's improper use of domestic surveillance was included in Article 2 paragraph (2) of the impeachment articles against him.)

According to Kelley, these congressional limits on the presidency, in turn, led "some very creative people" in the White House and the Department of Justice's Office of Legal Counsel (OLC) to fight back, in an attempt to foil or blunt these limits. In their view, these laws were legislative attempts to strip the president of his rightful powers. Prominent among those in the movement to preserve presidential power and champion the unitary executive doctrine were the founding members of the Federalist Society, nearly all of whom worked in the Nixon, Ford, and Reagan White Houses.

Restoring the Balance

In a democracy, such assertions of power [as President George W. Bush has made regarding Presidential Power] do not happen in a vacuum. They affect the careful balance of power in our system of government. The executive branch is not free to unilaterally change that balance; our Constitution requires legislative and judicial involvement to ensure public debate and oversight and to guard against centralization of power. . . .

The separation of powers is not a mere "technicality." It is the centerpiece of our Constitution, guarding us from the possibility of a monarchy (or worse). This balance must be restored.

Bob Barr,
"Bush's Signing Statements Are a Real Danger,"
ROLL CALL, *July 18, 2006.*

The unitary executive doctrine arises out of a theory called "departmentalism," or "coordinate construction." According to legal scholars Christopher Yoo, Steven Calabresi, and Anthony Colangelo, the coordinate construction approach "holds that all three branches of the federal government have the power and duty to interpret the Constitution." According to this theory, the president may (and indeed, must) interpret laws, equally as much as the courts.

The Unitary Executive Versus Judicial Supremacy

The coordinate construction theory counters the long-standing notion of "judicial supremacy," articulated by Supreme Court Chief Justice John Marshall in 1803, in the famous case of *Marbury v. Madison*, which held that the Court is the final arbiter of what is and is not the law. Marshall famously wrote there: "It is emphatically the province and duty of the judicial department to say what the law is."

Of course, the President has a duty not to undermine his own office, as University of Miami law professor A. Michael Froomkin notes. And, as Kelley points out, the President is bound by his oath of office and the "Take Care clause" to preserve, protect, and defend the Constitution and to "take care" that the laws are faithfully executed. And those duties require, in turn, that the President interpret what is, and is not constitutional, at least when overseeing the actions of executive agencies.

However, Bush's recent actions make it clear that he interprets the coordinate construction approach extremely aggressively. In his view, and the view of his Administration, that doctrine gives him license to overrule and bypass Congress or the courts, based on his own interpretations of the Constitution—even where that violates long-established laws and treaties, counters recent legislation that he has himself signed, or (as shown by recent developments in the [2004] Padilla case) involves offering a federal court contradictory justifications for a detention. . . .

This is a form of presidential rebellion against Congress and the courts, and possibly a violation of President Bush's oath of office, as well.

After all, can it be possible that that oath means that the President must uphold the Constitution only as he construes it—and not as the federal courts do?

And can it be possible that the oath means that the President need not uphold laws he simply doesn't like—even though they were validly passed by Congress and signed into law by him? . . .

The Unitary Executive Doctrine Violates the Separation of Powers

The President does not have unlimited executive authority, not even as Commander-in-Chief of the military. Our government was purposely created with power split between three branches, not concentrated in one.

Separation of powers, then, is not simply a talisman: It is the foundation of our system. James Madison wrote in The Federalist Papers, No. 47, that:

> The accumulation of all powers, legislative, executive, and judiciary, in the same hands, whether of one, a few, or many, and whether hereditary, self-appointed, or elective, may justly be pronounced the very definition of tyranny.

Another early American, George Nicholas, eloquently articulated the concept of "power divided" in one of his letters:

> The most effectual guard which has yet been discovered against the abuse of power, is the division of it. It is our happiness to have a constitution which contains within it a sufficient limitation to the power granted by it, and also a proper division of that power. But no constitution affords any real security to liberty unless it is considered as sacred and preserved inviolate; because that security can only arise from an actual and not from a nominal limitation and division of power.

Yet it seems a nominal limitation and division of power—with real power concentrated solely in the "unitary executive"—is exactly what President Bush seeks. His signing statements make the point quite clearly, and his overt refusal to follow the laws illustrates that point: In Bush's view, there is no actual limitation or division of power; it all resides in the executive.

Thomas Paine wrote in *Common Sense*:

> In America, the law is king. For as in absolute governments the King is law, so in free countries the law ought to be king; and there ought to be no other.

The unitary executive doctrine conflicts with Paine's principle—one that is fundamental to our constitutional system. If

Bush can ignore or evade laws, then the law is no longer king. Americans need to decide whether we are still a country of laws—and if we are, we need to decide whether a President who has determined to ignore or evade the law has not acted in a manner contrary to his trust as President and subversive of constitutional government.

> *"Jerry Miller ... became the 200th person exonerated by postconviction DNA testing. 200 people arrested, prosecuted, convicted, and sent to prison for years (14 of whom had been sentenced to death), eventually to have their innocence established by scientific proof."*

DNA Testing Proves the Legal System Is Flawed

Ezekiel Edwards

Ezekiel Edwards is a staff attorney with the Innocence Project, a nonprofit legal clinic and criminal justice resource center. He focuses on eyewitness identification reform. He contributes to the DMI Blog of the Drum Major Institute for Public Policy. In this viewpoint, Edwards contends that two hundred people exonerated of crimes after DNA testing is a troubling fact in a system that incarcerates 2.3 million people. He argues that such travesties of justice must be used to generate urgent reform to prevent future wrongful convictions.

As you read, consider the following questions:

1. How many of the two hundred people exonerated by post-conviction DNA testing had been sentenced to death? How many total years of prison time did these two hundred wrongfully convicted persons serve?

2. In what types of crime is there locatable DNA evidence, and enough of it, appropriate for testing to determine a defendant's innocence or guilt?

3. What mistake proven by DNA evidence was a contributing (or sole) factor in 77 percent of the two hundred wrongful convictions?

How can you simultaneously be one of the unluckiest and luckiest men in America? Ask Jerry Miller, who yesterday [April 3, 2007] became the 200th person exonerated by post-conviction DNA testing. 200 people arrested, prosecuted, convicted, and sent to prison for years (14 of whom had been sentenced to death), eventually to have their innocence established by scientific proof. 200 people who served a total of 2,475 years in prison, almost one million nights, for crimes they did not commit.

When Jerry Miller was 22 years old, the police picked him up after an officer said he resembled a composite sketch of a Chicago rapist. He was tried and convicted on the basis of the victim's subsequent misidentification, and served 24 years in prison before being released last year on parole. Since his release, he has lived as a registered sex offender, required to wear an electronic monitoring device at all times and prohibited from being alone with children or leaving his job for lunch.

For more than a quarter of a century, he maintained his innocence.

The Lessons of Injustice

People often tell me they can't imagine anything worse than spending years or decades in prison for a crime someone else committed. The only thing worse would be to endure the horror of wrongful conviction and not have it count for something—to have society fail to learn the lessons of injustice and reform the system to prevent it from happening to anyone else.

The 200 DNA exonerations nationwide give us irrefutable scientific proof of the flaws in the criminal justice system. . . .

We are in a race against time to test evidence before it is destroyed and to prove the truth before one of our clients spends another day behind bars. And we are in a race against time to fix the system before one more innocent person is swept off the streets, forcibly separated from his family and robbed of his freedom.

Barry Scheck, "On the 200th DNA Exoneration in the U.S.,"
The Huffington Post, April 22, 2007. www.huffingtonpost.com.

Through representation by the Innocence Project, Mr. Miller was able to secure a court order for testing DNA evidence in his case. The results: none of the forensic evidence came from Mr. Miller.

Tip of the Iceberg

Sadly, Mr. Miller's case is not unusual. Just since 2000, there have been 135 DNA-based exonerations. There have been 27 in Illinois alone. And this is just the tip of the iceberg, considering that in many of the older cases where there was DNA evidence, it has been lost, destroyed, or consumed by original testing.

More disturbingly, the vast majority of crimes do not involve forensic evidence. Take robbery cases, for example: there are far more robbery cases than murder or rape cases; they are highly susceptible to misidentification; and they almost never involve forensic evidence, meaning that there are thousands of prisoners who are precluded from ever even having the chance to scientifically establish their innocence. So, despite the 200 exonerations, these cases are only a sliver of the nation's "innocence" cases, falling into a small category of almost exclusively murder and rape cases in which there was DNA evidence, and enough of it, and locatable, and which a court deemed appropriate for testing. This would be troubling in any criminal justice system, but none more so than in a country with 2.3 million people behind bars.

As for the 200 exonerations, Barry Scheck, co-founder of the Innocence Project, wrote in a blog on the Huffington Post [website] that "these 200 people are a remarkably diverse group—they include a rich man's son in Oklahoma, homeless people, school teachers, day laborers, athletes and military veterans. But mostly they are African-American men without money to hire good lawyers (or, sometimes, any lawyers)."

Learning from the Travesties

It is not enough to recognize and lament such travesties of our criminal justice system; we must learn from these cases and use them to generate urgent reform throughout the system to prevent future wrongful convictions. As a result of these 200 cases, we know now, for instance, that in 77% of the 200 wrongful convictions proven by DNA evidence (including Mr. Miller's), mistaken eyewitness identification was a contributing (or sole) factor. Other common causes are forensic science errors (from simple mistakes to outright fraud), which played a role in nearly two-thirds of the wrongful convictions, and false confessions (as the result of coercive interrogations or defendants' limited mental capabilities), which existed in 25%.

Correcting these causes will not only protect the innocent from being arrested, but also from being harmed by the real perpetrator. Each time someone is wrongfully convicted, it means the actual culprit remains free. Indeed, in at least 30% of the 200 cases, DNA has led to the identification of the true perpetrator.

DNA Testing to Prove Innocence

As Scheck notes, implementation of these critical reforms has already begun: "Dozens of cities and states have changed their eyewitness identification procedures to make them more accurate, 500 jurisdictions now record interrogations to prevent false confessions, the federal government has implemented important crime lab standards and 40 states now grant prisoners access to DNA testing that can prove their innocence. But it's not enough. The Innocence Project receives thousands of letters a year from prisoners and their families, detailing flawed investigations and trials that were predestined to convict the wrong person."

It will not be long until we reach 300, or 500, perhaps 700 exonerations, since present-day reforms can do nothing to help innocent victims of past wrongs currently languishing in prison. But the sooner each state, each police department, each prosecutor's office, each legislature, embraces reform within our criminal justice system, the sooner we will witness a decline in the number of wrongful convictions, and the longer it will take before we are discussing the 1,000th exoneration. While innocent people remain in jail doing time unjustly, time is of the essence for justice to be done.

"DNA evidence is difficult to challenge in the courtroom because most people think it is virtually infallible. It is not just jurors, fed on a media diet of CSI-style fantasies, who think so. Most members of the academic and legal community believe it as well. . . . While there is no doubt that DNA testing rests on a stronger scientific foundation than many other forensic disciplines, recent events have proven that DNA evidence is hardly infallible."

DNA Testing Does Not Prove the Legal System Is Flawed

William C. Thompson

William C. Thompson is professor and chair of the Department of Criminology, Law and Society, School of Social Ecology, University of California, Irvine. He writes about the strengths and limitations of various types of evidence and about the ability of lay juries to evaluate evidence. In this viewpoint, Thompson contends that DNA evidence, despite its reputation as being "vir-

William C. Thompson, "Tarnish on the 'Gold Standard': Recent Problems in Forensic DNA Testing," *Champion Magazine*, January–February 2006, p. 10. Reproduced by permission.

tually infallible," is not. He cites numerous studies and investigations documenting DNA testing errors throughout the country.

As you read, consider the following questions:

1. The author reports that DNA testing errors have been popping up all over the country. What are some of the causes the author cites for many of the documented DNA testing mistakes?

2. Most problems with DNA testing are due to inadvertent mistakes, according to the author, though some DNA analysts have been fired for falsification of results. Name some of the agencies the author cites where analysts were fired for scientific misconduct?

3. According to Thompson, what are some reasons for DNA analysts' temptation to fake controls designed to detect contamination in DNA testing?

D NA evidence has long been called "the gold standard" of forensic science. Most people believe it is virtually infallible—that it either produces the right result or no result. But this belief is difficult to square with news stories about errors in DNA testing. An extraordinary number of problems related to forensic DNA evidence have come to light. Consider, for example, the following:

- The Houston Police Department (HPD) shut down the DNA and serology section of its crime laboratory in early 2003 after a television exposé revealed serious deficiencies in the lab's procedures, deficiencies that were confirmed by subsequent investigations. Two men who were falsely incriminated by botched lab work have been released after subsequent DNA testing proved their innocence. In dozens of cases, DNA retests by independent laboratories have failed to confirm the conclusions of the HPD lab. The DNA lab remains closed while an outside investigation continues.

- In Virginia, post-conviction DNA testing in the high-profile case of Earl Washington, Jr. (who was falsely convicted of capital murder and came within hours of execution) contradicted DNA tests on the same samples performed earlier by the State Division of Forensic Sciences. An outside investigation concluded that the state lab had botched the analysis of the case, failing to follow proper procedures and misinterpreting its own test results. The outside investigators called for, and the governor ordered, a broader investigation of the lab to determine whether these problems are endemic. Problematic test procedures and misleading testimony have also come to light in two additional capital cases handled by the state lab.

- In 2004, an investigation by the *Seattle Post-Intelligencer* documented 23 DNA testing errors in serious criminal cases handled by the Washington State Patrol laboratory.

- In North Carolina, the *Winston-Salem Journal* [in 2005] published a series of articles documenting numerous DNA testing errors by the North Carolina State Bureau of Investigation.

- The Illinois State Police [in 2005] cancelled a contract with Bode Technology Group, one of the largest independent DNA labs in the country, expressing "outrage" over poor quality work.

- [In 2005] LabCorp, another large independent lab, [was] accused of botching DNA paternity tests.

While these scandals are bad enough, the problems with DNA evidence do not end there. A close look at the field shows that DNA testing errors have been popping up all over the country. Many of the mistakes arise from cross-contamination or mislabeling of DNA samples. Problems of this type have been documented in Minnesota, North Carolina, Pennsylvania, Nevada, and California. Tellingly, one of the private labs hired to retest DNA evidence in cases that were botched by the Houston Police Department Crime Lab has itself produced false matches due to sample mix-ups. A particularly ominous sign of underlying problems is that accidental transfers of DNA among samples from different cases being processed by the same laboratory have produced several false "cold hits."

While most of the problems are due to inadvertent mistakes, a number of cases involving dishonesty have also come to light. DNA analysts have been fired for scientific misconduct, and specifically for falsification of test results, by a number of forensic laboratories, including labs operated by the FBI, Orchid-Cellmark (another large private DNA laboratory), the Office of the Chief Medical Examiner in New York City, and the United States Army. In all of these cases, the analysts were caught faking the results of control samples designed to detect instances in which cross-contamination of DNA samples has occurred.

So what is going on with DNA testing? How can we explain this sudden rash of problems with "the gold standard" of forensic science? How can a test that has long been advertised as virtually infallible produce so many errors? And what is behind the recent spate of dishonesty among DNA analysts? The answers to these questions are, in my view, interconnected. Some serious underlying problems with DNA testing that have existed for a long time are beginning to come to light. What we are seeing is not a sudden deterioration in the quality of DNA testing. It is the inevitable emergence and recognition of problems that existed all along but heretofore were successfully hidden. . . .

Bad Labs

One chronic problem that is now being recognized is the uneven quality of forensic DNA laboratories. Laboratories vary greatly in the care with which they validate their methods and the rigor with which they carry them out. Quality control and quality assurance procedures that are followed religiously in some labs are ignored or followed intermittently in others. . . .

Cross-Contamination and Sample Mix-Ups

Another problem now emerging into the light is an unexpectedly high rate of laboratory errors involving mix-up and cross-contamination of DNA samples. Errors of this type appear to be chronic and occur even at the best DNA labs. This is a problem that forensic scientists have largely managed to keep under wraps (perhaps because it is always embarrassing). Practitioners have long claimed that the rate of laboratory error in DNA testing is so low as to be negligible, but growing evidence suggests otherwise. . . .

Dishonest DNA Analysts

A third problem now emerging is dishonest DNA analysts who falsify test results. I suspect this third problem is closely related to the second problem: DNA analysts are faking test results to cover up errors arising from cross-contamination of DNA samples and sample mix-ups.

Given the unexpectedly high frequency of contamination in DNA testing, it is interesting, and not at all surprising, that the major form of fakery discovered to date involves control samples known as extraction blanks that are designed to detect contamination. These samples are supposed to contain no DNA. When they produce positive results, it indicates there was a problem—DNA somehow ended up in a sample where it did not belong. If that happened to a control sample, it could also have happened to other samples, so the analyst must throw out the whole test and start over.

The temptation to fake controls probably arises partly from production pressures and partly from the collision between the public image of DNA testing as infallible and the reality that it is easier than one might expect to botch a DNA test by cross-contaminating samples. Police and prosecutors have demanded DNA tests in an ever-expanding number of cases, putting pressure on labs to keep pace. Some labs have become high-tech sweatshops in which analysts are under pressure to maintain productivity. In this environment, the failure of a scientific control can be a big problem for a DNA analyst—it forces the analyst to redo the entire case, putting him or her behind schedule. . . .

Publicizing Problems

Defense lawyers are often among the first to know about problems in forensic laboratories because they encounter these problems when reviewing cases. While the primary obligation, on finding evidence of a lab problem, is of course to use that evidence to advocate effectively for the client, it is vital that defense lawyers also bring such evidence to the attention of the broader legal and scientific community so that underlying problems can be recognized and addressed. . . .

CSI-Style Fantasies

DNA evidence is difficult to challenge in the courtroom because most people think it is virtually infallible. It is not just jurors, fed on a media diet of CSI-style fantasies, who think so. Most members of the academic and legal community believe it as well. Even scholars who are critical of other areas of forensic identification science have argued that DNA is an exception—calling DNA testing "a model for scientifically sound identification science."

While there is no doubt that DNA testing rests on a stronger scientific foundation than many other forensic disciplines, recent events have proven that DNA evidence is hardly infallible. The solid scientific foundation for DNA testing is no guarantee that DNA tests will be carried out in a reliable manner that produces accurate results. Bad laboratory work is all too common and laboratory accidents and errors can occur even in good labs. Whether DNA evidence is trustworthy is a question that must be examined carefully in each case. And that challenging task falls ultimately on the shoulders of lawyers who represent clients incriminated by DNA tests.

Periodical Bibliography

The following articles have been selected to supplement the diverse views presented in this chapter.

Jeffrey Addicott "The Military Commissions Act: Congress Commits to the War on Terror," Forum, *Jurist Legal News and Research*, October 9, 2006, http://jurist.law.pitt.edu.

Amnesty International "United States of America, Military Commissions Act of 2006—Turning Bad Policy into Bad Law," September 29, 2006, www.amnesty .org.

Benjamin N. Cardozo "Facts on Post-Conviction DNA Exonerations," *Innocence Project*, www.innocenceproject.org.

Civil Liberties Online "Civil Liberties in Wartime: Supreme Court Case Law on the Protection of Civil Liberties during Times of War," *DukeLaw*, www.law.duke.edu/publiclaw.

B. Michael Dann, Valerie P. Hans, David H. Kaye "Can Jury Trial Innovations Improve Juror Understanding of DNA Evidence?" *Champion Magazine*, April 2007, www.nacdl.org.

Rhonda Riglesberger "A Flawed and Imperfect System," *Justice: Denied—The Magazine for the Wrongly Convicted*, www.justicedenied.org.

Matthew Robinson "Freedom in an Era of Terror: A Critical Analysis of the USA Patriot Act," *Justice Policy Journal*, vol. 4, no. 1, Spring 2007.

William S. Sessions "DNA Evidence and the Death Penalty," *Jurist*, May 30, 2007. http://jurist.law.pitt.edu.

Leon H. Wolf "An Objection Without Merit—Examining the Furor Over Presidential Signing Statements," *RedState*, www.redstate.com.

OPPOSING VIEWPOINTS® SERIES

CHAPTER *2*

Does the Judicial System Work?

Chapter Preface

The courtrooms of the United States, at every level of government, are public forums where issues of innocence and guilt are presented for judgment. In the courtroom setting, it is the responsibility of jurors to determine innocence or guilt and of the judge to impose a sentence. The judge has sentencing discretion within certain congressionally mandated advisory guidelines. Jurors receive instruction from the judge regarding which facts are in dispute and on points of law. The jury has the power to acquit in disregard of the instructions on the law given by the trial judge. This seldom-employed right is known as jury nullification and its application continues to be a matter of debate among legal scholars.

The U.S. legal system is adversarial. The prosecuting attorney attempts to prove the defendant's guilt, while the defense attorney acts to protect the defendant's legal rights and seeks out and presents evidence that may exonerate the defendant of charges or negotiates a plea bargain with the prosecutor on the defendant's behalf.

Though fewer than 10 percent of legal cases ever make it to a jury trial, U.S. courtroom dockets remain overcrowded, and the fairness and impartiality of the judicial system is a matter of frequent discussion. Judges must operate within a climate of sometimes adverse political pressure, media scrutiny, and public criticism.

According to Mark Harrison, who as of 2007 chairs the American Bar Association's Joint Commission to Evaluate the Model Code of Judicial Conduct, "an independent, impartial judiciary is indispensable to our system of justice. Equally important is the confidence of the public in the independence, integrity, and impartiality of our judiciary as an institution."

Roger Warren, former California trial judge and as of 2007 president of the National Center for State Courts, argues that "unfair personal attacks on judges, and electoral campaigns by special-interest groups to unseat judges with whose judicial decisions they disagree, unduly interfere with judicial independence and are inappropriate means of securing judicial accountability."

Traditionally, it has been the judiciary itself that is responsible for enforcement of ethical conduct. However, critics of the judicial system contend that the only way to ensure independence and restore confidence in the courts is through judicial accountability.

Republican Senator Charles Grassley of Iowa is concerned that "the judiciary hasn't done enough to reassure the public that it is doing all that it can to address what are perceived to be cracks in the system." He is calling for creation of an Office of Inspector General to oversee the U.S. judiciary. He has introduced legislation titled the "Judicial Transparency and Ethics Enhancement Act of 2007." This bill, if passed, "would amend the federal judicial code to establish the Office of Inspector General for the Judicial Branch of the U.S. government." The inspector general would be responsible for conducting investigations of alleged misconduct in the judicial branch, including the U.S. Supreme Court; conducting and supervising audits and investigations; and preventing and detecting waste, fraud, and abuse.

Andrew Cohen, writing in the *Washington Post* when the bill was first introduced in 2006, expressed a concern of many who oppose such legislation: "The bill, if it makes it into law, will be used by some creepy judicial inspector general sometime to go after some federal judge somewhere who has done nothing wrong but interpret the Bill of Rights in a manner that the inspector general doesn't happen to agree with."

Retired Supreme Court Justice Sandra Day O'Connor, speaking at Georgetown University in 2006, warned: "It takes a lot of degeneration before a country falls into dictatorship, but we should avoid these ends by avoiding these beginnings."

Efforts to balance judicial independence and accountability are ongoing, and this contentious issue promises to continue to be central in the debates on the integrity of the U.S. legal system. In chapter 2, various authors present their views on certain aspects of the judicial system and how well it upholds the principle of equal protection under the law.

> "Despite its shortcomings, one of the reasons this country has a bona fide law enforcement system with the ability to investigate and expose vast financial and political corruption is the power of the federal grand jury."

Grand Jury Powers Are Needed in Criminal Investigations

Peter F. Vaira

Peter Vaira is a former federal prosecutor, as of 2007 associated with the Philadelphia-based law firm of Vaira and Riley. The firm handles complex civil litigation and white-collar criminal defense in both federal and state courts throughout the United States. Vaira has served as the sole independent hearing officer for the Laborers' International Union of North America (LIUNA), a position created by an agreement between the Department of Justice and the union to initiate a process to remove the influence of organized crime on the union. In this viewpoint, Vaira contends that grand jury powers are a necessary investigative tool of prosecutors seeking to enforce the law.

As you read, consider the following questions:

1. According to Vaira, what was the original purpose of the grand jury as it came to the American colonies from England?

2. How many citizens comprise a federal grand jury? Where are their names drawn from?

3. According to Vaira, is hearsay evidence admissible in a grand jury hearing? If a subpoenaed witness refuses to appear, what might the person be charged with?

The federal grand jury is the backbone of the federal prosecution efforts. There is a lot of myth about the grand jury, a lot of platitudes issued by federal prosecutors, as well as criticism from legal scholars and the defense bar. Despite all the rhetoric, the grand jury is an institution that is not going to be radically changed without a constitutional amendment, which is very unlikely.

The original 13 states felt so strongly about the need for the grand jury that they insisted on its insertion as the Fifth Amendment to the newly drafted Constitution. The Fifth Amendment requires that a grand jury return all felony charges. It is ironic that today [as of 2007], a majority of the states have either abolished the grand jury or significantly modified its use after the Supreme Court held that the grand jury requirement for felony charges was inapplicable to the states. . . .

The original purpose of the grand jury, as it came to the American colonies from England, was to act as an independent bulwark between the king (or the prosecutor) and the citizen. As one court said, "the grand jury is a sword and a shield; sword because it is a terror to criminals and a shield because it is the protection of the innocent against unjust prosecution," as said in *United States v. Cox.* . . .

Times have changed, and even the Supreme Court has frankly stated that the grand jury does not live up to that original purpose of serving as an independent body. "The grand jury may not always serve its historic role as a protective bulwark standing solidly between the ordinary citizen and an overzealous prosecutor," as the court wrote in *United States v. Dionisio*. Although the grand jury was created to be independent of any branch of the government, for all practical purposes the grand jury has become the instrument of the prosecutor.

Despite its shortcomings, there are those, including this writer, who would not want the grand jury replaced with some adversary probable-cause system, or would want the vast power of the grand jury to issue subpoenas to be watered down. Despite its shortcomings, one of the reasons this country has a bona fide law enforcement system with the ability to investigate and expose vast financial and political corruption, is the power of the federal grand jury. In the Watergate scandal, despite all his stonewalling, President Richard M. Nixon conceded his office would respect the grand jury subpoena.

This does not mean that the grand jury is without flaws. One must recognize it for what it is today, a powerful law enforcement tool with limited rights for the witnesses and defendants.

What Is the Grand Jury

The federal grand jury is comprised of 23 citizens selected at random from the voters' rolls. The grand jury has the power to inquire into possible violations of the law based upon information from investigators, or tips, rumors and hearsay. There is no probable cause requirement for the grand jury to initiate an inquiry or issue subpoenas. A grand jury is impaneled to sit for 18 months. The term of the grand jury may be extended for a period of up to six months.

The prosecutor makes the decision as to what areas to investigate. In most instances, the federal agencies supply subjects for investigation as a result of their own agency inquiries. The grand jury is used to subpoena records from business entities or persons or to subpoena persons for personal testimony.

The prosecutor makes the decision of which persons and what records to subpoena. It is very rare that the grand jury is given any discretion as to who will be subpoenaed and what documents will be requested. There is no recorded instance of a grand jury countermanding a prosecutor's decision to subpoena certain persons or certain documents.

In order to cause the grand jury to return an indictment, the prosecutors must present sufficient evidence to demonstrate there is probable cause to believe that a felony has been committed by a person, and that the person should stand trial for that charge. Sixteen grand jurors are required for a quorum. The vote of 12 grand jurors is required for the return of the indictment. . . .

The defense counsel is not entitled to appear before the grand jury, and the prosecutor is not obligated to present the grand jury with any briefs or arguments written by defense counsel. Nor is the prosecution required to call any witnesses suggested by the defense counsel. The defense counsel is not permitted to review the evidence presented to the grand jury if his client would appear and testify. The targeted potential defendant may appear before the grand jury if he elects to testify; however, in today's grand jury procedure few experienced defense counsel would permit their clients to do so.

If an indictment is returned the defendant is not entitled to review the grand jury transcript, except for the transcript of the testimony of witnesses who testify at trial, and his own testimony if he appeared.

Grand jury sessions are secret; only the jurors, the prosecutor, the witness, and a stenographer are present. No coun-

U.S. Constitution: Fifth Amendment

No person shall be held to answer for a capital, or otherwise infamous crime, unless on a presentment or indictment of a Grand Jury, except in cases arising in the land or naval forces, or in the Militia, when in actual service in time of War or public danger; nor shall any person be subject for the same offence to be twice put in jeopardy of life or limb; nor shall be compelled in any criminal case to be a witness against himself, nor be deprived of life, liberty, or property, without due process of law; nor shall private property be taken for public use, without just compensation.

U.S. Constitution, Fifth Amendment.
http://caselaw.lp.findlaw.com/data/constitution/amendment05/.

sel for the witness can be present. A witness may leave [the] room to consult with counsel. Until 1979, grand jury sessions were not recorded. There were so many allegations of abuse that the Supreme Court amended Fed. R. Crim. P. 6(e)(1) to require all proceedings before the grand jury be transcribed by an official court reporter.

Grand jurors may be replaced by the court at any time during the term of the grand jury. There is no limit on the number of grand jurors that may be replaced.

A matter heard by one grand jury may be continued before a successor grand jury. This transfer may be accomplished without court order. The second grand jury is not required to hear all the direct testimony heard by the first grand jury; much of first grand jury testimony may be presented to the second grand jury by reading the jurors transcripts of the prior testimony.

The grand jury may continue to investigate a matter after indictment if . . . its purpose [is] to investigate non-indicted persons, or other crimes arising out of those circumstances.

Courts will not interfere with post-indictment grand jury proceedings as long as the dominant purpose of them is not to discover facts relating to a pending prosecution.

Evidence that May Be Heard

There are no formal rules of evidence for the grand jury. Hearsay is perfectly admissible. In the early part of the twentieth century up until the 1960s, the usual method of obtaining an indictment was to place one Federal investigative agent on the witness stand to relate the results of his investigation. The agent would summarize his witness interviews, review of documents, factual observances, and any statements obtained from the defendant. This was perfectly acceptable. . . .

In the early 1960s, the Organized Crime Section of the U.S. Department of Justice, under Attorney General Robert Kennedy, began to use the grand jury as an investigative tool. Numerous persons who were witnesses or parties to criminal activity were subpoenaed before the grand jury. Many of those witnesses had refused to be interviewed by federal agents.

The Organized Crime Section was responsible for the wide use of the grand jury as an investigative tool that we know today. In the 1970s, U.S. attorneys' offices in New Jersey, Chicago and Philadelphia began major investigations of political corruption using the grand jury. The use of the grand jury to obtain testimony from recalcitrant witnesses increased after the passage of the use immunity statute.

As a practical matter, a great deal of evidence presented to the grand jury is hearsay. In 1972, the 2nd U.S. Circuit Court of Appeals warned prosecutors that although hearsay evidence was perfectly admissible, the grand jurors were not to be misled that the evidence they were hearing was the firsthand knowledge of the witness. Today [in 2007], with the use of extensive grand jury investigations and the appearance of multiple witnesses, the excessive use of hearsay evidence is no longer a credible issue. The grand jury may subpoena a witness to provide voice exemplars, handwriting samples, or hair samples and fingerprints.

Requiring Witnesses to Produce Evidence

One cannot overstate the power of the grand jury to issue *subpoenas duces tecum* [a command by the grand jury that requires a witness to produce evidence]. Realistically this power is virtually unlimited. The grand jury does not have to demonstrate the relevance of the subpoena duces tecum nor does it need to demonstrate probable cause to issue a subpoena duces tecum.

For example, a prosecutor may suspect that a certain corporation or public entity is being used by its officers for fraudulent purposes. He may have some intelligence information supporting his suspicion, but that is not necessary. Without more, the prosecutor can simply issue a grand jury subpoena to the organization for financial records. There is no credible challenge that can be made to quash the subpoena on the grounds that there are no grounds to initiate the investigation.

A court may quash or modify a grand jury subpoena duces tecum if it is unreasonable or oppressive in scope. However, courts give a great deal of deference to the grand jury. Subpoenas have been upheld for massive amounts of records dating back five years or more. For instance, a subpoena duces tecum in an antitrust investigation may request documents filling hundreds of filing drawers. Realistically the grand jury does not examine these documents. The documents are given to federal agents for examination, who report to the grand jury if any incriminating information is discovered. . . .

There are few grounds to quash a subpoena for a personal appearance before the grand jury. A witness may not appeal the subpoena directly, but must disobey [the] subpoena and challenge the subpoena at a contempt hearing.

An exception to the rule is that a witness may demonstrate a physical inability to appear by a motion to quash. Upon receipt of a subpoena to testify, the witness should request to be notified of his or her status. Upon the witnesses' request, the Department of Justice will inform the witness if he or she is a subject or target.

A subject is a person whose conduct is within the scope of the grand jury's investigation. A target is a person as to whom the prosecutor or the grand jury has substantial evidence linking him or her to the commission of a crime and, who, in the judgment of the prosecutor, is a putative defendant. Failure to notify a witness of his or her target status is not grounds for setting aside the indictment.

The witness may assert certain testimonial privileges, and the notification to the prosecutor of the existence of certain privileges may excuse the witness from appearing. Department of Justice internal regulations permit the prosecutor to excuse a witness from appearing if the witness notifies the prosecutor that he intends to assert the Fifth Amendment to all questions. The assertion of the attorney-client privilege or other privileges based upon factual premises will usually require a motion to quash to be heard by the court to substantiate the facts underlying the privilege.

The power to compel compliance with grand jury subpoena lies with the court. A witness who refuses to appear may be held in criminal contempt or civil contempt.

> *"A defendant who is subject to indictment by grand jury is denied the right to present evidence to explain or contradict the charge, has no right to appear or to have the assistance of counsel, and may not confront and cross-examine the witnesses against him."*

Grand Jury Procedures Harm the Accused

Richard Alexander and Sheldon Portman

Richard Alexander and Sheldon Portman are, as of 2007, with the law firm of Alexander Hawes. Alexander is a member of the Board of Governors of The State Bar of California and the Board of Governors of Consumer Attorneys of California; he is also the president of the Santa Clara County Bar Association. Portman is a former public defender and recipient of the 1982 Reginald Heber Smith Award of the National Legal Aid and Defender Association. In this viewpoint, Alexander and Portman contend that the grand jury has ceased to fulfill its original role and has become subject to incapacitating manipulation and abuse.

As you read, consider the following questions:

1. Where did the grand jury originate and for what purpose, according to Alexander and Portman?

2. Alexander and Portman contend that the grand jury process is no longer effective in protecting individuals against arbitrary prosecutions. Which "landmark study" do they cite and what was its conclusion?

3. When a defendant is charged by information gained at a preliminary hearing, according to the authors, who judges the evidence?

Historically, the grand jury has been looked upon as a suitable device for protecting the weak or unpopular from judicial harassment or politically motivated prosecutions. The grand jury is supposed to function as a body of neighbors who aid the state in bringing criminals to justice while protecting the innocent from unjust accusation. However, both the grand jury and the criminal information have ceased to fulfill these original role-obligations and have become increasingly subject to incapacitating manipulation and abuse. All of the major recent studies conclude that the grand jury has become, in effect, a rubber stamp of the prosecutor and not the check on his power that it is required to be.

Origin of the Grand Jury System

The origins of the institution of the grand jury are obscure. In some form it was found early in all the Teutonic peoples, including the Anglo-Saxons before the Norman Conquest. Forms of the grand jury have also been traced in Scandinavian countries where jurors came to determine both law and fact. The grand jury originated in Anglo-American law with the summoning of a group of townspeople before a public official to answer questions under oath.

In 1166, the Crown first established the criminal grand jury, a body of twelve knights, or other freemen whose function was to accuse those who, according to public knowledge, had committed crimes. The purpose was to give to the central government the benefit of local knowledge in the apprehension of those who violated the king's peace. Witnesses as such were not heard before this body. The use of accusing juries provided for in the Assizes of Clarendon (1166) and Northampton (1176), closely resembles the modern grand jury in personnel, duties and powers. During the thirteenth and early part of the fourteenth centuries, the grand jurors themselves served as petit jurors in the same matters in which they presented indictments. Not until the eventual separation of the grand jury and petit jury did the function of accusation become clearly defined and did Crown witnesses come to be examined in secret before the grand jury. By the time of the appearance of le graunde inquest in 1368, the grand jury had acquired the powers and duties of the present-day grand jury and it has not changed materially since that time. . . .

Origin of the System of Prosecution by Information

Parallel to the development of the grand jury was the development of the criminal information. The use of the criminal information dates at least from the time of Edward I (1272–1307). Other evidence tracing the origins of the criminal information makes clear that its history and use in certain times and cases is almost as old as that of the indictment. Like its counterpart, the grand jury, the criminal information was also subject to manipulation and abuse from early times. . . .

Both the grand jury and the criminal information found their way to America, and both are used here today [as of 2007].

A Prosecutor's "Shiniest Tool"

Grand juries operate in secret. They work with the prosecutor; they hear witnesses; and there is no judge in the room. Normal rules of evidence don't apply. Grand juries wield enormous power. They can issue subpoenas (which are written by prosecutors) to require witnesses to come forward and testify or to produce books, papers, documents, or other things. Shrouded in secrecy and fortified with enormous power, the grand jury is a kind of American version of the Star Chamber, or perhaps more aptly put, a Starr Chamber [Kenneth Starr, in the Office of Independent Counsel, worked to impeach President Bill Clinton].

Ironically, grand juries are provided for in the Bill of Rights. Pursuant to Amendment V: "No person shall be held to answer for a capital, or otherwise infamous crime, unless on a presentment or indictment of a grand jury." It is ironic that grand juries are contained in provisions about rights, because today grand juries are largely the tool of prosecutors. There's the famous quip that a "prosecutor can get a grand jury to indict a ham sandwich." And that might be putting it too mildly—it applies to any sandwich, not just ham. A grand jury is one of the shiniest tools in the prosecutor's tools shed.

Daniel Solove, "Beware the Grand Jury," Balkinization, *July 7, 2005.*
http://balkin.blogspot.com/2005/07/beware-grand-jury.html.

Criticism of the Grand Jury System

In [the United States] numerous studies undertaken to assess the efficacy of the grand jury have all concluded that it is no longer effective in protecting individuals against arbitrary prosecutions, and that it no longer exercises the independent judgment required by due process. The landmark study in this century was conducted by Dean Wayne Morse of the University of Oregon Law School. After an exhaustive study of 7,414 indictments and extensive questionnaires sent to prosecutors and judges, Dean Morse concluded:

> Grand juries are likely to be a fifth wheel in the administration of criminal justice in that they tend to stamp with approval, and often uncritically, the wishes of the prosecuting attorney. At best the grand jury tends to duplicate the work of the committing magistrate and prosecutor.

Dean Morse found that in only 5.15 percent of the cases initiated by the prosecutor in which he expressed an opinion was there a disagreement between the opinion of the prosecutors and the grand jury dispositions. Similarly, the National Commission on Law Observance and Enforcement concluded:

> The grand jury usually degenerates into a rubber stamp wielded by the prosecuting officer according to the dictates of his own sense of propriety and justice. [The grand jury] has ceased to perform or be needed for the function for which it was established.

Most recently [as of 2007], Weinberg and Weinberg, in discussing preliminary hearings in federal courts, concluded with respect to grand juries:

> The grand jury is not a proper body to reach an "independent judicial determination" of probable cause. Its determination is unlikely to be "judicial" because it is composed of laymen, whose sole guidance on legal questions will normally come from the prosecutor. Its determination is also unlikely to be "independent" in most cases because, in practice, the prosecutor's influence is usually controlling.

The Second Circuit recently [as of 2007] described the grand jury as basically "a law enforcement agency" a conclusion supported by numerous studies. Most recently William J. Campbell, Senior Judge, United States District Court for the Northern District of Illinois, recommended that the grand jury be completely eliminated and replaced by a procedure encompassing an advisory preliminary examination before a judicial officer to determine probable cause. . . .

In *People v. Elliot* the purpose of the preliminary examination process was described in the following language:

> The preliminary examination is not merely a pre-trial hearing. "The purpose of the preliminary hearing is to weed out groundless or unsupported charges of grave offenses, and to relieve the accused of the degradation and the expense of a criminal trial. Many an unjustifiable prosecution is stopped at that point, where the lack of probable cause is clearly disclosed." . . .

Of equal, if not greater, import to our citizens is the fact that a preliminary examination provides them protection from the ignominy and expense of going to trial unless there has been an evidentiary hearing and a holding that sufficient evidence exists to justify trial.

In a prosecution by information, California law requires that there be an independent evidentiary determination of probable cause in an adversary proceeding before trial but no equivalent right is granted to an accused who is prosecuted by grand jury indictment. Where an indictment is issued by the grand jury, the accused is not afforded the safeguard of an independent judicial evaluation of the evidence.

"Devoid of Fairness"

Indictment by grand jury affords none of the fundamental rights provided in a preliminary examination. Unless he is called as a witness, the defendant has neither the right to appear and present evidence to the grand jury nor to confront witnesses against him. Only the district attorney, the attorney general or special counsel may appear and present evidence. Even if called as a witness, a defendant may not have the assistance of counsel to advise him. Although the grand jury may require the district attorney to issue process for defense witnesses when it "has reason to believe that such evidence exists," this provision is of little practical value since the proceedings are held in secret with no notice to a defendant. Furthermore, as indicated by the opening statement of Penal Code Section 939.7, the grand jury is "not required to hear evidence for the defendant," and thus may reject such evidence at the very outset. Without hearing the evidence in the first place, the opportunity to determine whether evidence exists to "explain away the charge" is in effect foreclosed, virtually assuring the finding of an indictment under Penal Code Section 939.8 on the basis of "unexplained or uncontradicted" evidence.

In support of its finding, the grand jury is required to "receive none but evidence that would be admissible over objection at the trial of a criminal action. . . ." In determining what is admissible evidence, the grand jury may ask for the advice of the judge or district attorney. However, unless such advice is requested, the judge is excluded from the session, leaving the jury to rely upon the prosecutor to advise it. These contradictions have been the object of criticism by one commentator who has observed:

> When the function of indictment is mated with the responsibility of determining the character of the evidence that supports it, and with the right to exclude all evidence which could explain or contradict, the result is not proper. In short, it is both derogatory of the jury's basic purpose and devoid of fairness.

Thus, a defendant who is subject to indictment by grand jury is denied the right to present evidence to explain or contradict the charge, has no right to appear or to have the assistance of counsel, and may not confront and cross-examine the witnesses against him. On the other hand, a defendant charged by information has all of these rights in addition to the fact that, unlike the grand jury indictment process, the evidence is judged by a neutral and detached magistrate capable of independently evaluating the admissibility of that evidence.

> *"As long as peremptory challenges are around . . . the way in which one experiences one's religion—no matter what the religion happens to be—seems as good a target as any for the exercise of such challenges."*

Peremptory Challenges Based on Religion Should Be Allowed

Sherry F. Colb

Sherry F. Colb is a professor at Rutgers Law School in Newark, NJ, and a columnist with FindLaw.Com, a Web site that publishes legal news and commentary. In this viewpoint, Colb acknowledges that jury selection based on the issue of religious affiliation may eventually be ruled by the U.S. Supreme Court a constitutionally forbidden discrimination. However, she argues, it is the strength of religious involvement—the level of "religiosity," rather than simple affiliation—that is sufficient for a peremptory challenge to a prospective juror.

As you read, consider the following questions:

1. There are two types of challenges used in jury selection to strike a potential juror. According to
   Colb, what are they and how do they differ?

2. In Colb's view, why is discrimination on the basis
   of race and sex prohibited in jury selection?

3. Colb compares "religiosity" with "gender-osity" and
   "racial-osity," as ways an individual may experience
   one's self and one's identity differently from other
   members of one's religion, one's sex, or one's race.
   What examples does she offer?

Prior to every trial, whether criminal or civil, the judge and
attorneys consider a large group of potential jurors. They
ultimately settle on twelve (or fewer) who will be the jury in
the case (along with any alternates).

Though different jurisdictions handle the elimination of
jurors in distinct ways, there are ordinarily two vehicles
through which one or the other side might strike a potential
juror from the pool. One is for-cause challenges. The other is
peremptory challenges. . . .

Peremptory challenges regularly rest on impressionistic
(and often wildly inaccurate) overgeneralizations about people
who share a common trait. In other words, they often rely on
stereotypes. Challenges for cause, by contrast, must rest on ar-
ticulable, persuasive, and legitimate grounds.

Permissible and Impermissible Stereotyping

When an attorney exercises peremptory challenges, she uses
her discretion to reject potential jurors who are not, objectively speaking, objectionable. These people do not bring any
obvious bias to the courtroom, and an attempt to eliminate
them for cause would almost certainly fail.

The lawyer might nonetheless have a bad feeling about the
person, dislike him personally or otherwise oppose him for

reasons that—if actually articulated—would sound foolish or even offensive. Peremptory challenges thus provide each attorney with the freedom to be downright arbitrary, a limited number of times, to help craft a desired jury.

The U.S. Supreme Court, however, has placed boundaries around this freedom. . . .

The rationale behind prohibiting some exercises of discretion is that the Equal Protection Clause of the Fourteenth Amendment protects people against invidious [calculated] discrimination. Though any arbitrary decision "discriminates" between people for questionable reasons, some kinds of discrimination—on the basis of race or sex, for example—trigger particulary harsh judgment under the Equal Protection Clause.

Because of a history of persecution on the basis of these categories, the Court has held that no one serving her government as a juror should have to tolerate being the victim of such discrimination. . . .

Is Religion a Prohibited Ground?

The Supreme Court has yet to rule on whether striking a juror based on religious affiliation triggers the special treatment so far reserved for race and sex. If an attorney eliminates John Doe from the pool because Doe is Catholic, does that strike violate the Constitution?

Neither federal nor state courts have reached a consensus on this question, and the U.S. Supreme Court may eventually have to resolve it definitively. There is good reason to expect, however, that discrimination on the basis of religious affiliation will be added to the list of forbidden categories, because it has historically been characterized by some of the same sorts of abuse identified with race and sex discrimination. . . .

Is Religiosity, As Opposed to Religious Affiliation, a Prohibited Ground?

In *United States v. Dejesus*, Jerry Dejesus was convicted of possession of a weapon by a convicted felon. Dejesus was sen-

Religion Is a Choice: Peremptory Challenge Should Be Allowed

Religion-based peremptory challenges should be allowed because they are distinguishable from those based on race and gender. First, while race and gender are immutable qualities, religion is a choice; therefore, it is more indicative of a person's belief system and values.

Second, this country does not have a history of religious discrimination in the jury-selection process that is analogous to its history of racial or gender discrimination in jury selection. Third, the alternative, challenge-for-cause system would interfere with providing litigants an impartial jury, diminish public confidence in the court system, enable lying jurors to manipulate the voir dire process, and leave too much discretion in the hands of the court as opposed to the litigants.

Kelly Lina Kuljol,
*"Where Did Florida Go Wrong? Why Religion-Based Peremptory
Challenges Withstand Constitutional Scrutiny,"*
Stetson Law Review, *vol. 32, no. 1, fall 2002.*

tenced to 110 months in prison, along with three years of supervised release and special assessment of $100. On appeal, Dejesus argued, among other things, that his conviction should be overturned because the prosecutor impermissibly exercised peremptory challenges based on a prohibited ground, namely religiosity.

The government countered that it did not eliminate jurors based on their religious affiliation—Christian versus Jewish versus Muslim versus Hindu. Instead, it struck jurors who were highly committed to the practice of religion.

In the case of one juror, his responses to a questionnaire (distributed to everyone in the jury pool) indicated that his life included a high degree of religious involvement and revolved around the church. Based on this information, the prosecutor concluded that the juror might be excessively compassionate (and not sufficiently judgmental) towards a guilty defendant.

The Court of Appeals considered and rejected the defendant's argument that such stereotyping on the basis of religiosity or religious commitment violates the Equal Protection Clause in the same manner as stereotyping based on race or sex. It held that even if religious affiliation itself were a prohibited ground for, peremptory challenges—a question on which [the] court withheld judgment—the government's use of religiosity to strike jurors would not fall into the same prohibited category.

Religious Affiliation Versus Religious Commitment

At first glance, it might seem that the Court of Appeals was drawing a distinction without a difference. After all, part of what it often means to be affiliated with a particular religious group is to observe relgious commandments associated with membership in that group.

On this reasoning, it would appear disingenuous to say, for example, that a prosecutor could not eliminate Jews from a jury but could eliminate everyone who refrains from working on the Saturday Sabbath and who refrains from eating or drinking on the holiday of Yom Kippur.

On closer examination, however, the distinction may be more compelling than it seems. To eliminate people who celebrate the Jewish Sabbath and Yom Kippur is likely in fact to be a pretext for eliminating Jews. If so, then a prohibition on peremptory challenges based on religious affiliation would suffice to invalidate such peremptory challenges, for a judge could easily see through the subterfuge.

If a judge determines, however, that an attorney has sincerely applied a criterion of religiosity rather than pretextually applying a criterion of religious affiliation, then a very different (and far less historically tainted) sort of discrimination may be taking place.

Consider the following example. The prosecutor collects jury questionnaires and notes that seven potential jurors have responded "yes" to the question "Does religion play a central role in your every day life?" The prosecutor does not know from their responses whether the writers are Catholic or Protestant or Muslim or Jewish (or some combination of these or other religious affiliations). Nonetheless, she wishes to eliminate them because she believes that the greater one's commitment to religion, the less sympathetic one is to the harsh punishment of criminal offenders.

The prosecutor may well be mistaken in her assumption. One might expect that very religious people would be more, rather than less, inclined to judge misconduct harshly. The more religious a person is, one might assume (without researching the empirical question), the more willing she is to accept and enforce legal requirements that might seem excessively intrusive or moralistic.

Both assumptions might be mistaken, of course, and religiosity may have nothing to do with one's disposition toward the criminal law. But speculating about whether it does seems more like speculating about people who grew up in the Northeast, or people who enjoy watching television, than it does like stereotyping Jews or Muslims.

The question of how one practices one's religion (as opposed to the question of what one's religion is) is a question about personal preferences and priorities, and that is exactly the sort of question that we expect attorneys to ask in jury selection.

Analogue to Race and Gender:
When Jurors May Permissibly Be Challenged

One way to think about religiosity is to compare it to what I would call "gender-osity" or "racial-osity," which I would define as a heightened commitment to one's identity as a member of one's gender or race.

In the case of gender, a potential juror might describe himself as a member of the "men's movement" who believes that women have encroached on male prerogatives and have turned masculine creatures into effeminate losers.

Another might describe herself as a woman whose greatest loyalty is to women and who considers herself a woman first and a citizen second. She might spend most or all of her time engaging in activism connected to her commitment to women's empowerment.

To eliminate such people from the jury pool would not reflect gender stereotyping so much as a desire to clear the jury of people holding strong ideological commitments through which they might filter their understanding of the litigated facts.

Similarly, the elimination of a white supremacist or one who identifies himself as "very white," and as racially committed to white people, should not raise the same red flags as the elimination of people based on race. Nor should the elimination of people who consider their primary commitment to be to the betterment of life for African-Americans, and who consider the U.S. government to be deeply prejudiced against African-Americans.

To be religious, gender-ous, or racial-ous is to experience one's self and one's identity in a way that might distinguish one from other members of one's religion, one's sex, or one's race. It might also generate similarities to people who are otherwise very different in their beliefs and commitments but whose identities center, respectively, on the same dimensions of their lives.

The Future: Will We See an End to Peremptory Challenges?

It may be that ultimately, peremptory challenges will fail to survive in the face of the growing number of categories that trigger suspicion under the Equal Protection Clause. Indeed, the more often an attorney is forced [to] articulate a non-invidious reason for a peremptory challenge, the less freedom the attorney truly has to strike jurors for "any" reason, or for no reason at all. . . .

As long as peremptory challenges are around, moreover, the way in which one experiences one's religion—no matter what that religion happens to be—seems as good a target as any for the exercise of such challenges. Perhaps the speculation, as I have suggested, is often incorrect, but incorrect stereotypes are not the same as invidious ones.

> *"While challenges based on mere affiliation with a particular religious denomination may violate the Constitution, challenges based on a juror's 'heightened religious involvement' do not. . . . You may be struck from a jury not for being a Christian, a Jew, or a Muslim, but only for being a rather devout Christian, Jew, or Muslim."*

Peremptory Challenges Based on Religion Should Not Be Allowed

Robert T. Miller

Robert T. Miller is a member of the New York State Bar Association and a research fellow in Law at the Columbia University Law School. In this viewpoint, Miller explains the process of jury selection and the history of peremptory challenges. He contends that the Court of Appeals decision holding that it is rational for a prosecutor to challenge a juror who reveals "a rather consuming propensity to experience the world through a prism of religious beliefs," is yet "another defeat for those who would like to prevent the denuding of the American public square."

As you read, consider the following questions:

1. Until 1986, peremptory challenges were allowed in jury selection without requirement to show cause. What Supreme Court decision changed this custom?

2. According to the Court, what clause of the U.S. Constitution is violated by peremptory challenges based on a juror's race?

3. What is a Batson hearing, according to Miller? In what federal case did the Court decide that challenges to potential jurors based on affiliation with a particular religion were in violation of the Constitution?

As anyone who has been through the process knows, selecting a jury is a complex business. The court starts with a large pool of prospective jurors and the judge and lawyers for the parties interview them, rejecting some and choosing others until they have a full panel, usually twelve. If, in the course of this process, a lawyer thinks that there is a good reason to exclude a prospective juror (e.g., that the juror would favor one side or the other), the lawyer may object to this person "for cause"; if the judge agrees, the juror will be excused. In addition, each side in the case is entitled to a limited number of "peremptory challenges" (the exact number of these depends on the nature and complexity of the case), which allow the lawyers to strike jurors without having to state any reason whatsoever. Writing in 1769, [the English jurist] William Blackstone described this ancient practice of the common law as being typical of "that tenderness and humanity for which our English laws are justly famous." According to Blackstone, we must all be "sensible what sudden impressions and unaccountable prejudices we are apt to conceive upon the bare looks and gestures of another," and so a man on trial for his life should be given the chance to keep off the jury someone "against whom he has conceived a prejudice, even without being able to assign a reason for his dislike."

Challenges on Race and Sex

So the practice continued in the United States—until 1986, when the United States Supreme Court decided, in *Batson v. Kentucky*, that litigants should not be permitted to exercise peremptory challenges based on a juror's race. Such discrimination, the Court said, would violate the equal protection clause of the Fourteenth Amendment. Given the history of racism in the United States, and especially because in some Southern states litigants might collude to exclude blacks from juries entirely, there was something to be said for *Batson*. But the Supreme Court did not stop there. In *J.E.B. v. Alabama* (1994), the Court decided that sex, too, would be an impermissible basis for the use of peremptory challenges. There was much less justification for this decision, not only because litigants were less likely to try to exclude women as a class, but also because there are usually too many women among potential jurors for litigants to remove them all using their limited number of peremptory challenges. But regardless, the Supreme Court had spoken.

One consequence of this development is the so-called *Batson* hearing, a proceeding in which, after a lawyer has peremptorily challenged a juror, the other side to the litigation, if it suspects that the strike was based on race or sex, may contest the challenge and force the opposing counsel to explain a basis for the challenge unrelated to race and sex. Of course, since peremptory challenges were originally intended to be exercisable for any reason or for no reason, *Batson* hearings can be absurd, as lawyers try to explain the unexplainable and give good reasons for actions that they were allowed to take without good reasons. Moreover, requiring courts to decide which explanations for the use of peremptory strikes are acceptable has produced a significant amount of legal mischief.

"Heightened Religious Involvement"

Which brings us to a lawyer striking jurors on the basis of their religious practices. In a recent federal case in New Jersey, *United States v. De Jesus*, the defense counsel demanded a *Batson* hearing after the prosecutor used peremptory challenges to strike two black jurors. The prosecutor then explained that he struck the jurors, not on the basis of their race, but because of their "heightened religious involvement." One of the jurors had said that he participated in civic activities at his church, read the *Christian Book Dispatcher*, taught Sunday school, and sang in the church choir, the other juror had stated that he was an officer and trustee of his church and that he read the Bible and related literature. The prosecutor concluded that these jurors would have difficulty sitting in judgment on another human being and so would be reluctant to convict.

This reasoning is in itself rather curious, since the usual stereotype about religious people is just the opposite—namely; that they tend to impose their values on others. Indeed, many secular people suppose that those who read the Bible are eager to sit in judgement, to say with St. Paul, "Those who do such things deserve death" (Romans 1:32). But however this may be, the judge accepted the prosecutor's explanation, and the Court of Appeals for the Third Circuit affirmed, holding that, while challenges based on mere affiliation with a particular religious denomination may violate the Constitution, challenges based on a juror's "heightened religious involvement" do not. Quoting the trial judge, the Court of Appeals said that it is rational for a prosecutor to challenge a juror who reveals "a rather consuming propensity to experience the world through a prism of religious beliefs." You may thus be struck from a jury not for being a Christian, a Jew, or a Muslim, but only for being a rather devout Christian, Jew, or Muslim.

Everyone recognizes that some forms of prejudice are worse than others, the basis for such distinctions generally being historical. In the United States, for example, where we have a long history of both de facto and de jure racial discrimination, we rightly think that such prejudice is gravely wrong and should be ruthlessly eliminated from our society. But beyond this and a handful of similar verities, people are apt to disagree about the relative moral badness of various forms of prejudice. One's judgments about such things will depend strongly on the details of one's moral philosophy. . . .

A Victory for Liberalism

When the Court of Appeals for the Third Circuit in the *De Jesus* case suggested that peremptory challenges made on the basis of mere religious affiliation would violate the equal protection clause, it did so because secular liberalism regards all religions as equally good (or at least equal); it would thus be wrong, on the liberal view of things, to allow a litigant to discriminate on such a basis. Here we have liberalism trying to speak some words to celebrate religion. But when it comes to a person displaying a "propensity to experience the world through a prism of religious beliefs," constitutional protections apparently disappear. As soon as religion becomes a serious competitor to liberal ideology, liberals are prepared to act against it. Religion that can be domesticated deserves toleration; religion that cannot be domesticated must be destroyed, and so the court allowed peremptory strikes on the basis of "heightened religious involvement."

Though the number of devoutly religious persons excluded from juries will probably be small, the symbolic significance of *De Jesus* is enormous. Call it yet another victory for the liberalism of personal autonomy in constitutional law—and another defeat for those who would like to prevent the denuding of the American public square.

> "Conservative activists. . .summoned the
> raw rage of the Christian right. . .and
> likened judges to communists, terrorists
> and murderers."

The Religious Right Attempts to Influence Judges

Max Blumenthal

In the following viewpoint, author Max Blumenthal recounts the scene at the "Confronting the Judicial War on Faith" conference. Blumenthal describes the conservative view that "judicial tyranny" must be stopped with the Constitution Restoration Act. This bill would authorize Congress to impeach judges who fail to abide by "the standard of good behavior" and states that the refusal to acknowledge "God as the sovereign source of law, liberty, or government" could result in judges' impeachment.

As you read, consider the following questions:

1. What remedies have conservative activists suggested for judicial tyranny, as cited by Blumenthal?
2. What sparked the reignition of the judicial impeachment campaign?

3. According to the author, what case remains the "flashpoint" for the right-wing activists?

Michael Schwartz must have thought I was just another attendee of the "Confronting the Judicial War on Faith" conference. I approached the chief of staff of Oklahoma's GOP [The Republican party is sometimes referred to as the Grand Old Party] Senator Tom Coburn outside the conference in downtown Washington last Thursday afternoon after he spoke there. Before I could introduce myself, he turned to me and another observer with a crooked smile and exclaimed, "I'm a radical! I'm a real extremist. I don't want to impeach judges. I want to impale them!"

For two days, on April 7 and 8 [2005], conservative activists and top GOP staffers summoned the raw rage of the Christian right following the Terri Schiavo affair, and likened judges to communists, terrorists and murderers. The remedies they suggested for what they termed "judicial tyranny" ranged from the mass impeachment of judges to their physical elimination.

The speakers included embattled House majority leader Tom DeLay, conservative matriarch Phyllis Schlafly and failed Republican senatorial candidate Alan Keyes. Like a performance artist, Keyes riled the crowd up, mixing animadversions on constitutional law with sudden, stentorian salvos against judges. "Ronald Reagan said the Soviet Union was the focus of evil during the cold war. I believe that the judiciary is the focus of evil in our society today," Keyes declared, slapping the lectern for emphasis.

At a banquet the previous evening, the Constitution Party's 2004 presidential candidate, Michael Peroutka, called the removal of Terri Schiavo's feeding tube "an act of terror in broad daylight aided and abetted by the police under the authority of the governor." Red-faced and sweating profusely, Peroutka added, "This was the very definition of state-

109

sponsored terror." Edwin Vieira, a lawyer and author of How to Dethrone the Imperial Judiciary, went even further, suggesting during a panel discussion that Joseph Stalin offered the best method for reining in the Supreme Court. "He had a slogan," Vieira said, "and it worked very well for him whenever he ran into difficulty: 'No man, no problem.'"

The complete Stalin quote is, "Death solves all problems: no man, no problem."

The threatening tenor of the conference speakers was a calculated tactic. As Gary Cass, the director of Rev. D. James Kennedy's lobbying front, the Center for Reclaiming America, explained, they are arousing the anger of their base in order to harness it politically. The rising tide of threats against judges "is understandable," Cass told me, "but we have to take the opportunity to channel that into a constitutional solution."

Cass's "solution" is the "Constitution Restoration Act," a bill relentlessly promoted during the conference that authorizes Congress to impeach judges who fail to abide by "the standard of good behavior" required by the Constitution. If they refuse to acknowledge "God as the sovereign source of law, liberty, or government," or rely in any way on international law in their rulings, judges also invite impeachment. In essence, the bill would turn judges' gavels into mere instruments of "The Hammer," Tom DeLay, and Christian-right cadres.

Conference speakers framed the Constitution Restoration Act in pseudo-populist terms—the only means of controlling a branch of government hijacked by a haughty liberal aristocracy against the will of the American people. As Michael Schwartz remarked during a panel discussion, "The Supreme Court says we have the right to kill babies and the right to commit buggery. They say the people have no right to express themselves, that the people have no right to make laws. Until we have a court that reflects a majority," Schwartz continued, his voice rising steadily, "it is a sick and sad joke that we have a Constitution here."

The right wing claims that judges should reflect majority opinion. But what is the majority opinion? After DeLay and Senate majority leader Bill Frist passed special bills ordering federal courts to consider the reinsertion of Terri Schiavo's feeding tube, according to a Gallup poll, Congress's public approval rating sank to 37 percent, lower than at any time since shortly after Republicans impeached President Bill Clinton. Meanwhile, 66 percent of respondents to a March 23 CBS News poll thought Schiavo's feeding tube should be removed. The notion that the Christian right's agenda is playing well in Peoria must be accepted on faith alone.

The recent right-wing fixation on impeaching judges was conceptualized by David Barton, Republican consultant and vice chairman of the Texas GOP. In 1996 Barton published a handbook called *Impeachment: Restraining an Overactive Judiciary*, which was timed to coincide with Tom DeLay's bid for legislation authorizing Congress to impeach judges. "The judges need to be intimidated," DeLay told reporters that year.

In 1989 Barton published a book titled *The Myth of Separation*, which proclaims, "This book proves that the separation of church and state is a myth." The Baptist Joint Committee on Public Affairs, in a critique of his 1995 documentary *America's Godly Heritage*, stated that it was "laced with exaggerations, half-truths, and misstatements of fact." Barton is on the board of advisers of the Providence Foundation, a Christian Reconstructionist group that promotes the idea that biblical law should be instituted in America. In 1991 Barton spoke at a Colorado retreat sponsored by Pastor Pete Peters, an adherent of racist Christian Identity theology with well-established neo-Nazi ties. During the 2004 presidential campaign, the Republican National Committee hired him as a paid consultant for "evangelical outreach." The RNC sponsored more than 300 events for him.

DeLay's bill, based on Barton's writings, failed due to lack of GOP support. But the judicial impeachment campaign was reignited six years later when a federal court ordered the removal of then-Alabama Supreme Court Chief Justice Roy Moore's Ten Commandments monument from courthouse grounds. In February 2004 a group of about twenty-five enraged ministers and movement leaders gathered in Dallas to plot a new response. The Constitution Restoration Act was the result. According to Moore, he was a principal author, along with Herb Titus, the former dean of Pat Robertson's Regent University law school, and Howard Phillips, a veteran third-party activist whose US Taxpayers' Party served as a vehicle for the antigovernment militia movement during the 1990s. All three men stalked the halls of the downtown Marriott last Thursday and Friday [in 2005].

In the Senate the bill was sponsored by Richard Shelby, a senator from Roy Moore's home state; among the co-sponsors is Senator Sam Brownback of Kansas, who is contemplating a run for the Republican nomination for President. The bill was introduced on March 3 [2005], before the Terri Schiavo affair erupted, before Florida Circuit Judge George Greer ordered the removal of her feeding tube and before he became the poster-child for the right's judicial impeachment campaign.

Now, according to Howard Phillips in a speech to the conference, his "good friend" Wisconsin GOP Representative James Sensenbrenner is planning to hold hearings on the Constitution Restoration Act in the House. DeLay, who appeared on a big screen during a Thursday morning session to call for the removal of "a judiciary run amok," has put his name on the act as the House sponsor.

The Schiavo case remains the flashpoint for the right. That was apparent at a Thursday evening banquet honoring the lead attorney for Terri Schiavo's parents, David Gibbs. After a breathless introduction from Peroutka, who called the removal of Schiavo's feeding tube "an act of terror," Gibbs confidently strode to the lectern while a crowd of about 100 regaled him with a thunderous standing ovation. Baby-faced, with his hair molded tightly against his scalp and clad in a well-tailored navy blue suit, Gibbs maintained a cool disposition during his speech, presenting a sharp visual contrast to the wildly gesticulating, bedraggled figures who held the microphone throughout most of the conference. But Gibbs's impeccable appearance and measured tone were not enough to mask the lurid nature of his speech.

First, Gibbs suggested that Schiavo fell into a persistent vegetative state not because of an eating disorder but as the result of "some form of strangulation or abuse at the hands of her husband, possibly." Then, Gibbs asserted that after Schiavo's parents were awarded millions of dollars by the state to provide for her care, Michael Schiavo "began moving against the family to kill his wife." These claims, however, did not hold up in court because, as Gibbs explained, "a judge that never went to see [Schiavo] was the judge who made the decision that her life did not matter."

As members of the audience gasped, Gibbs painted a vivid portrait of Schiavo in her hospital bed. "Terri Schiavo was as alive as anyone you see sitting here," he said. "She liked my voice. It was loud and deep and she would roll over and try to talk back." But after Judge Greer "literally ordered her barbaric death," everything changed.

Gibbs described his visit to Schiavo's hospital room after her feeding tube had been removed. Schiavo lay in bed "with her eyes sunken deep in her head. . .she was skeletal," Gibbs recounted. "Then she turned to her mother suddenly, like she wanted to speak, and she just started sobbing." By now, members of the audience were crying.

As soon as he left the stage, one of the event's planners asked all the men in the room to get down on the floor and pray. With no other choice, I moved my plastic-upholstered chair aside, took to my hands and knees and listened as plaintive voices arose all around me with prayers for Schiavo's parents and maledictions against judicial tyranny. A saccharine version of Pachelbel's *Canon* emanating from the player piano in the hotel lobby seeped through the banquet hall's open doors, suffusing the ceremony with a dreamlike atmosphere. When I finally dared to look up from the ground, I realized that my head was only inches from an enormous posterior belonging to William Dannemeyer, the former congressman who once issued a letter to his colleagues listing twenty-four people with some connection to Bill Clinton who died "under other than natural circumstances."

As the conference attendees filed out of the banquet hall and into the rain-flecked night, mostly silent except for the few who were still sobbing, they seemed prepared to do anything—absolutely anything—against judges. "I want to impale them!" as Michael Schwartz told me.

"This isn't Colombia. This isn't drug lords terrorizing the judiciary. It's America," Florida Judge George Greer declared recently. Greer remains under police guard.

On Monday, April 11 [2005], at Senator Frist's invitation, David Barton will lead him and other senators on an evening tour of the Capitol, offering "a fresh perspective on our nation's religious heritage."

| "The judiciary is fast becoming enemy
No. 1 in the culture wars—and the side
wearing the black robes is losing."

Political Attacks Threaten
Judicial Independence

Bert Brandenburg

*Bert Brandenburg is the executive director of the Justice at Stake
Campaign, a nonpartisan national organization working for fair
and impartial courts. In this viewpoint, Brandenburg argues
that the controversial court decision in the Terri Schiavo case
boosted a rising common culture of attacks on the independence
and legitimacy of the judiciary. The author contends that members of Congress increasingly seek to reverse or forestall court decisions they do not agree with by such measures as eliminating
jurisdiction over important constitutional cases. Brandenburg
points to the age of cable television and blogs that has contrib-
uted to the "instant outrage" that he argues had led to congressional manipulation of court jurisdiction.*

As you read, consider the following questions:

1. In the author's opinion, how do hostile members of
   Congress seek to reverse or forestall court decisions
   they do not like?

2. According to Brandenburg, what powers do the provision, buried within the Real ID Act, give to the secretary of homeland security? Is this open to court review?

3. The author contends that there is an "intimidation campaign" under way against judges who make controversial decisions. What are some of the attempts to punish judges that the author cites?

Was Terri Schiavo's piteous ordeal a victory for the rule of law? After all, interest groups and the politicians they pressured were trumped by the courts. The macabre circus that arose around Mrs. Schiavo's case counted for nothing: Pinellas County judge George W. Greer issued a steady series of rulings despite being targeted for electoral defeat and impeachment, compared to Joseph Mengele and other Nazis, and even threatened with death. The public didn't buy legislation that sought to rig the case for Schiavo's parents. "If nothing else," wrote a *New York Times* analysis, "this series of decisions vindicated the one conception of American judicial power."

But that isn't quite right. In fact, the Schiavo episode spells trouble ahead for the courts that protect our rights. The judiciary is fast becoming enemy No. 1 in the culture wars—and the side wearing the black robes is losing. The anguish over Mrs. Schiavo's nightmare is boosting a rising common culture of attacks on the independence and legitimacy of our courts. In Washington and far beyond the Beltway, this new war on the courts is being waged through legislation and political intimidation, fueled by special interest campaigns of rage.

Consider the bill that sailed through Congress on Palm Sunday (2005), hustling Mrs. Schiavo's case into federal courts. Legal purists cringed at the politics of crafting jurisdiction to reach a desired result. But the For the Relief of the Parents of Theresa Marie Schiavo Act was just another day at the office for legislators working to manipulate the jurisdiction of our

Strong and Independent Judiciary is Vital

The framers knew it was critical that the judicial branch of government operate in a strong and independent manner to keep the other two branches in check. They also knew that it was imperative that the judiciary be insulated from improper political pressure. To this end, while the Constitution provided that all federal judges were to be appointed by the president with the advance and consent of the Senate, they were also granted life tenure. This was intended to give them a measure of freedom to decide cases and controversies, and to develop a fair and uniform body of national law, without fear of political reaction.

Likewise it is essential to the effective functioning of democratic governments in the states that their judiciaries be strong and independent. State governments are largely based upon the federal model with each state having a legislative and executive branch. Thus, the traditional checking role of the state judiciary is vital to the proper functioning of state governments. Moreover, state courts have broader jurisdiction than their federal counterparts, and they handle approximately 90 percent of the nation's litigation. This gives state trial and appellate courts a greater impact on the daily life of our citizens and a very substantial role in shaping the country's collective rule of law.

Angela Mazzarelli, "Independence of State Judiciary Is Vital,"
New York Law Journal, *January 22, 2007.*

courts to achieve political ends. Hostile members of Congress increasingly seek to reverse or forestall decisions they don't like by eliminating jurisdiction over important constitutional cases, shuffling selected lawsuits between state and federal courts, and choking off the discretion of judges to weigh evidence and law.

Straight Off Talk Radio

These efforts often come straight off the talk-radio dial. Last year, for example, even as the federal courts mulled litigation involving the Pledge of Allegiance, the House of Representatives was passing a measure to forbid courts from ever hearing such a case in the first place. As the debate raged over a courthouse display of the Ten Commandments, a measure was written to deny federal courts the power to hear *any* suit involving a governmental official's "acknowledgment of God as the sovereign source of law, liberty, or government." And the recent California marriage decision reignited efforts to amend the U.S. Constitution in order to deny state courts the ability to interpret their own state constitutions.

These efforts at court-stripping don't just represent just good wedge-issue politics; increasingly, they have become the law of the land. The USA Patriot Act reduced judicial discretion to review law-enforcement efforts to detain suspects, monitor private Internet communications, obtain certain personal records and share wiretaps with intelligence agencies. The 2003 "Feeney Amendment"—protested strongly by Chief Justice William Rehnquist—sharply limited the ability of federal judges to issue sentences below federal guidelines in order to set punishments that fit the crime.

As they grow more confident, enemies of the courts are growing more extreme. Buried within the Real ID Act (signed into law May 11, 2005,) is a provision that would swap martial law for the rule of law. The bill would give the secretary of homeland security unilateral power to waive any law on the books that might interfere with the building of border fences—including civil-rights and minimum-wage protections, and even criminal laws. Courts would be barred from ever reviewing the secretary's stroke of the pen.

Measures like these flow from a view of our courts as little more than enemy combatants. After the Supreme Court ruled that certain antiterrorism tactics violated the Bill of Rights, (former) attorney general Ashcroft accused it of endangering national security. During the Schiavo case, (former) House majority leader Tom DeLay warned that "no little judge sitting in a state district court in Florida is going to usurp the authority of Congress." And the latest best-selling screed against the judiciary—*Men in Black: How the Supreme Court Is Destroying America*—repeatedly accuses the courts of "tyranny" that make it "difficult to maintain a republic." Congressional leaders brag that they will "take no prisoners" in dealing with the courts and that "judges need to be intimidated."

This intimidation campaign is now well under way. A Reagan-appointed judge was recently hauled before a congressional committee to explain comments that weren't properly supportive of sentencing guidelines. There's a new effort to make impeachment into a respectable punishment for federal judges who make controversial decisions, exceed their jurisdiction, or consult foreign law in their deliberations. State judges have also seen a spike in impeachment threats: 39 from 2002 to 2004, almost double the previous three years.

The job of protecting our rights sometimes requires that our judges show a little steel. After the 1954 *Brown v. Board of Education* desegregation decision, lawmakers tried to impeach justices, abolish life tenure on the Supreme Court, and strip it of jurisdiction over public-education cases. When the Court struck down laws banning interracial marriage in 1968, opponents pointed to polls showing that more than 70 percent of Americans disapproved. In 1943, at the height of the global fight against fascism, the Court struck down laws requiring Jehovah's Witnesses to recite the Pledge of Allegiance.

The courts have survived these and other contretemps— including the *Bush v. Gore* firestorm. But in the age of cable television and blogs, instant outrage is getting easier to manufacture. . . .

Our courts now face nothing less than a permanent campaign—the kind political organizers and fundraisers lick their lips at, since there will always be controversial new cases to replenish the trough. This appetite for fresh outrage helps explain proposals to give parents more rights to litigate end-of-life disputes. After all, why would those who accuse judges of murder want to dump thousands more controversial cases into their laps? In the world of hardball politics, it turns out that losing in court can be a very good thing indeed.

Periodical Bibliography

The following articles have been selected to supplement the diverse views presented in this chapter.

Akron Beacon Journal	"Strategy of Liberty: The Supreme Court Now Must State for a Third Time Why Guantanamo Detainees Deserve Their Day in Federal Court," February 27, 2007.
Ashley Gauthier	"Secret Justice: Gag Orders—Good Judges, Denying Gags," *The News Media and the Law*, The Reporters Committee for Freedom of the Press, www.rcfp.org.
Tom Maguire	"Grand Jury Secrecy," *Just One Minute*, March 12, 2007, http://justoneminute.typepad.com.
Paul K. McMasters	"Too Much Secrecy Is a Challenge to Justice," First Amendment Center, December 18, 2005, www.firstamendmentcenter.org.
Monica Miller and Brian Bornstein	"Does Religion Predict Juror Decisions? Implications for Peremptory Challenges," Paper presented at the annual meeting of the *The Law and Society Association*, July 6, 2006, www.allacademic.com.
Patterico	"Is Jury Nullification Ever Appropriate?" *Patterico's Pontifications*, August 29, 2006, http://patterico.com.
Jane Pribek	"At Risk: Judicial Independence," *Wisconsin Law Journal*, August 24, 2005, www.wislawjournal.com.
Mike Renzulli	"Jury Nullification: Liberty's Last Hope," *Freedom's Phoenix*, May 15, 2007, www.freedomsphoenix.com.
USA Today	"O'Connor: Court Criticisms Unjustified," May 20, 2007, www.usatoday.org.

CHAPTER 3

Is the Criminal Justice System Fair?

Chapter Preface

Equal justice under the law is a foundational principle of the U.S. legal system. This cornerstone of U.S. democracy is reflected in the Declaration of Independence and in the United States Constitution, and it was a principle in twelve out of thirteen of the original colonies. It was not until 1963, however, that the Supreme Court decided that the constitutional right of assistance of counsel was applicable to each of the states under the due process clause of the Fourteenth Amendment. The Court ruled that the appointment of counsel for an indigent criminal defendant is a "fundamental right, essential to a fair trial."

Yet nearly half a century later, even in situations in which the life or death of the accused hangs in the balance, many legal scholars argue that equal justice is still an unfulfilled promise in many U.S. courtrooms. According to Bill Redick, director of the Tennessee Justice Project, a nonprofit organization committed to increasing the fairness and accuracy of the Tennessee indigent criminal justice system, "the outcome of death penalty trials cannot be trusted." Writing in the *Tennessean* in 2006, Redick contends: "We run the risk of executing defendants, not because they are the worst offenders, but because they have the worst lawyers." In Tennessee, as in many states, the majority of criminal defendants are indigent. When indigent defense is underfunded, critics argue, effective defense is not possible, and all too frequently legal counsel is limited to negotiating a plea agreement.

Throughout the U.S. legal system, fewer than 10 percent of defendants charged with a crime will bring the case to trial. Plea bargaining bypasses the due-process rights guaranteed in the Constitution. Some critics contend that this process of negotiation between the prosecution and defense replaces evidence as the main determinant of guilt or innocence.

"Plea bargaining has nothing to do with justice. It has to do with convenience, expediency, making the life of prosecutors and defense attorneys easier and more profitable. It is designed to avoid finding out the truth. It is designed to avoid hearing the defendant's story," according to Albert Alschuler, a professor of law and criminology at the University of Chicago, in a 2004 *Frontline* interview.

Another justice system critic, from the San Jose Silicon Valley NAACP, writing on the blog *The NAACP Speaks*, argues that "with overzealous prosecutors and inept defense attorneys polluting our justice system it would seem that our current principles of the legal profession have turned into idealistic rhetoric."

According to the American Bar Association, however, "plea bargaining is a necessary element of the United States criminal justice system. Properly negotiated and structured, plea agreements in general benefit defendants, the government, and the judiciary. In addition, the public benefits from plea-bargaining because plea agreements result in the conservation of public resources as well as the quick disposition of criminal cases."

Authors in chapter 3 explore the question of fairness in the U.S. legal system. The widespread practice of plea bargaining in every legal jurisdiction in this country continues to be a controversial aspect of the U.S. legal system. The debates on this and other issues relating to the principle of equal justice under the law is likely to have far-reaching effects on the administration of justice for years to come.

> *"Habeas corpus—the Great Writ—has been the pre-eminent safeguard of individual liberty for centuries by providing meaningful judicial review of executive action and ensuring that our government has complied with the Constitution and the laws of the United States."*

Habeas Corpus Is the Foundation of a Fair Justice System

Alberto J. Mora and Thomas R. Pickering

Alberto J. Mora is retired general counsel of the United States Navy. He received the 2006 Profiles in Courage Award for his efforts within the Defense Department to end coercive interrogation tactics at Guantanamo Bay prison camp, which he contends are unlawful. Thomas R. Pickering served as a career ambassador, the highest rank in the U.S. Foreign Service, in a diplomatic career spanning five decades. Both Mora and Pickering are members of the Council on Foreign Relations. In this viewpoint, the authors contend that the judicial branch's ability to consider

Alberto J. Mora and Thomas R. Pickering, "Act Attacks What America Is All About." *Albany Times Union* (Albany, NY), March 6, 2007, p. A9. Copyright © 2007 *Albany Times Union*. Reproduced by permission of the authors.

writs of habeas corpus is critical to its role of safeguarding civil liberties and should not be limited by the legislative branch.

As you read, consider the following questions:

1. In the authors' opinion, what is the function of a writ of habeas corpus?
2. What law has limited the courts' ability to hear habeas petitions filed by certain noncitizens?
3. According to the authors, how long have some prisoners at Guantanamo been held without a hearing?

For more than 200 years, the courts have served as the ultimate safeguard for our civil liberties. A critical part of this role has been the judicial branch's ability to consider writs of habeas corpus, through which people who have been imprisoned can challenge the decision to hold them in government custody. In this way, habeas corpus has provided an important check on executive power. However, because of a provision of the Military Commission Act, this fundamental role of the courts has been seriously reduced.

Habeas corpus—the Great Writ—has been the pre-eminent safeguard of individual liberty for centuries by providing meaningful judicial review of executive action and ensuring that our government has complied with the Constitution and the laws of the United States. Habeas review has always been most critical in cases of executive detention without charge because it provides prisoners a meaningful opportunity to contest their detention before a neutral decision maker.

In 2004, the Supreme Court held that the protections of habeas corpus extend to detainees at Guantanamo Bay, who may rely on them to challenge the lawfulness of their indefinite detentions. The Court noted that at its historical core, "the writ of habeas corpus has served as a means of reviewing the legality of Executive detention, and it is in that context that its protections have been strongest."

But the Military Commissions Act eliminates the federal courts' ability to hear habeas petitions filed by certain noncitizens detained by the United States at Guantanamo Bay and elsewhere. The U.S. Court of Appeals for the D.C. Circuit upheld this provision late last month and dismissed the lawsuits filed by many of the Guantanamo detainees.

Habeas Corpus Is Crucial

We fully recognize that our government must have the power to detain suspected foreign terrorists to protect national security. But removing the federal courts' ability to hear habeas corpus claims does not serve that goal. On the contrary, habeas corpus is crucial to ensure that the government's power to detain is exercised wisely, lawfully and consistently with American values. That is why we have joined with the Constitution Project's broad and bipartisan group of judges, former members of Congress, executive branch officials, scholars and others to urge Congress to restore federal court jurisdiction to hear these habeas corpus petitions. The unconventional nature of the "war on terrorism" makes habeas corpus more, not less, important. Unlike what is found in traditional conflicts, there is no clearly defined enemy, no identifiable battlefield and no foreseeable end to the fighting. The government claims the power to imprison individuals without charge indefinitely, potentially forever. It is essential there be a meaningful process to ensure the United States does not mistakenly deprive innocent people of their liberty. Habeas corpus provides that process.

We recognize the Military Commissions Act still enables the Guantanamo detainees to have hearings before a Combatant Status Review Tribunal, which is charged with determining whether the detainee is in fact an "enemy combatant." But unlike court hearings, the tribunal hearings rely on secret evidence, deny detainees the chance to obtain and present their own evidence, and allow the government to use evidence ob-

Lynchpin of Freedom

The writ of habeas corpus is actually the lynchpin of a free society. Take away this great writ and all other rights—such as freedom of speech, freedom of religion, freedom of the press, gun ownership, due process, trial by jury, and protection from unreasonable searches and seizures and cruel and unusual punishments—become meaningless.

The Framers considered the writ of habeas corpus so important that they specifically provided for its protection in the Constitution: "The privilege of the Writ of Habeas Corpus shall not be suspended, unless when in Cases of Rebellion or Invasion the public Safety may require it." As Alexander Hamilton put it, the writ of habeas corpus, along with the prohibition against ex post facto laws, "are perhaps greater securities to liberty" than any others in the Constitution. . . .

In the absence of the power of federal courts to issue writs of habeas corpus, all the other rights and guarantees in the Constitution and the Bill of Rights become dead letters. If there is no way to enforce the First Amendment, for example, through a writ of habeas corpus seeking the release from custody of a government critic, critical speech is inexorably suppressed. After all, how many newspaper editors, Internet critics, and war protesters would continue their criticism, knowing that other critics were languishing in some dark, perhaps even secret, detention camp without hope of challenging their detention in court through a writ of habeas corpus? . . .

[Americans'] indifference to the cancellation of the Great Writ—the writ of habeas corpus, the lynchpin of a free society—is an affront those who struggled for centuries to ensure its enshrinement and protection. . . .

Jacob G. Hornberger, "Habeas Corpus: The Lynchpin of Freedom,"
LewRockwell.com, October 12, 2006.

tained by coercive interrogation methods. While these tribunals have some utility, they cannot replace the critical role of habeas corpus.

The government has detained some Guantanamo prisoners for more than five years without giving them a meaningful opportunity to be heard. The United States cannot expect other nations to afford its citizens the basic guarantees provided by habeas corpus unless it provides those guarantees to others.

And in our constitutional system of checks and balances, it is unwise for the legislative branch to limit an established and traditional avenue of judicial review.

Repairing the Damage

Americans should be proud of their commitment to the rule of law and not diminish the protections it provides. Our country's detention policy has undermined its reputation around the world and has weakened support for the fight against terrorism. Restoring habeas corpus rights would help repair the damage and demonstrate U.S. commitment to a counterterrorism policy that is tough but also respects individual rights.

Congress should restore the habeas corpus rights that were eliminated by the Military Commissions Act, and President Bush should sign that bill into law.

"The Constitution does not make habeas corpus an absolute right that must be made available even to our avowed foreign enemies during war. . . . Neither the Geneva Convention nor any other international treaty or law supersedes the authority of our duly constituted government, in protecting its citizens, to suspend habeas corpus under such exigent circumstances."

Habeas Corpus Suspension Is a Necessary War-Time Power

Joseph Klein

Joseph Klein is the author of Global Deception: The UN's Stealth Assault on America's Freedom. *He is a columnist with FrontPage Magazine, an online conservative political magazine. In this viewpoint, Klein addresses the issue of suspension of habeas corpus, a right which he contends is not absolute and was never intended to be available to alien enemy combatants during wartime.*

Joseph Klein, "Affirming Our Constitution," *FrontPageMagazine.com*, February 26, 2007. Reproduced by permission.

As you read, consider the following questions:

1. Which law, enacted in 2006, contained provisions stripping habeas corpus rights?

2. During wartime, in Klein's view, who has power to determine alien detainee status?

3. Klein contends that the issue of public safety is at stake with regard to the rights of foreign enemies during war. What section of the Constitution deals with habeas corpus suspension?

The United States D.C. Circuit Court of Appeals upheld [in February 2007] the constitutionality of the habeas corpus-stripping provisions of the Military Commissions Act of 2006. Finally, we have witnessed an example of a court that understands its own limitations in fighting the fanatical terrorist enemies who pose the true threat to our Constitution.

Although its 2 to 1 majority decision was savagely attacked by the *New York Times* for putting "American liberty at the precipice," all that the Appeals Court actually did was to defer to the two elected branches of our government in deciding how best to handle alien enemy combatant detainees who are suspected terrorists.

The Supreme Court had ruled last year in *Hamdan v. Rumsfeld* that Congress—not the President alone—had the authority to establish the rules governing military tribunals. "Nothing prevents the President from returning to Congress to seek the authority he believes necessary," according to Justice Breyer's concurring opinion. The Supreme Court's Hamdan decision focused on the separation of powers involving the relative authority of the two political branches—Congress and the President. The Supreme Court ruled in favor of Congress's prerogatives under its legislative war making powers. The issue was solved when Congress passed the Military Commissions Act signed by President Bush into law last October. The President now has the authority that the Supreme

Court said he needed from Congress to proceed with his alien enemy combatant detention program. And Congress expressly intended this law to bar the federal courts from considering all pending and future habeas corpus petitions from alien detainees who are designated as unlawful enemy combatants. During wartime, that determination belongs to the President as commander-in-chief under guidelines established by Congress.

In short, Congress and the President are now on the same page—at least until the Democratic majority is able to repeal the law's restrictions on habeas corpus petitions to the benefit of the terrorists, as some are trying to do.

No Habeas without "Presence or Property"

The Appeals Court considered the history of the writ of habeas corpus, which was intended to afford prisoners the right to challenge their confinement but was not intended to be available to aliens "without presence or property within the United States." In determining whether the Guantanamo detention facility where the enemy combatants were being held was considered within the sovereign jurisdiction of the United States for this purpose, the Appeals Court again deferred to the judgment of Congress and the President as well as pointing out that Guantanamo is leased from the government of Cuba which retains sovereign jurisdiction over the territory.

We can expect an appeal to the Supreme Court. In addition to arguing that Guantanamo is under the operational control of the U.S. military, meaning that the detainees do have a presence in the U.S. for the purpose of being entitled to file a petition for a writ of habeas corpus, the appeal will most likely argue that a basic universal human right of the detainees has been violated when they are not allowed to file such a petition. In other words, invoking the Geneva Conventions and the talisman of international law once again, the terrorist civil liberties crowd will try to convince the Supreme

Take Habeas Off the Table

Sen. Lindsay Graham (R-S.C.)

"Why do we—I and others—want to take habeas off the table and replace it with something else? I don't believe judges should be making military decisions in a time of war. There is a reason the Germans and the Japanese and every other prisoner held by America have never gone to federal court and asked the judge to determine their status. This is not a role the judiciary should be playing. They are not trained to make those decisions. I believe very vehemently that the military of our country is better qualified to determine who an enemy combatant is over a federal judge. That is the way it has been, that is the way it should be, and, with my vote, that is the way it is going to be. . . .

"These trials impede the war effort. It allows a judge to take what has historically been a military function.

"To substitute a judge for the military in a time of war to determine something as basic as who our enemy is not only not necessary under our Constitution, it impedes the war effort, it is irresponsible, it needs to stop, and it should never have happened. I am confident Congress has the ability, if we choose to redefine the rights of an enemy combatant non-citizen, [to determine] what rights they have in a time of war."

R. Robin McDonald, "Debate over Habeas Rights Roils Senate,"
Fulton County Daily Report, October 11, 2006.

Court that the Military Commissions Act should be declared unconstitutional because its detention provisions defy international norms of 'civilized' conduct. Indeed, they just got a boost from a decision handed down by Canada's highest court on February 23, 2007, which struck down a law allowing the Canadian government to detain foreign-born terrorist suspects indefinitely while their deportations are under review. The United States program director for Amnesty International was quoted in the *New York Times* as saying that the Canadian decision should serve as a "wake-up call that reminds us that civilized people follow a simple and basic rule of law, that indefinite detention is under no circumstances acceptable."

Wake-Up Call

Well, here is a wake-up call for the terrorists' legal advocates. Our enemies invaded our homeland on 9/11 and killed 3,000 innocent people with their attacks on the World Trade Center and the Pentagon. Having already declared war against the United States, they are actively plotting more murderous invasions as we speak, and they have not been shy in saying so. They have broken every law of war and civilized conduct in the books and then some. The Constitution does not make habeas corpus an absolute right that must be made available even to our avowed foreign enemies during war. Article I, Section 9 of the Constitution says flatly that "the privilege of the writ of habeas corpus shall not be suspended, unless when in cases of rebellion or invasion the public safety may require it." Neither the Geneva Convention nor any other international treaty or law supersedes the authority of our duly constituted government, in protecting its citizens, to suspend habeas corpus under such exigent cicumtances. . . .

We need not decide whether Abraham Lincoln had been correct in suspending habeas corpus rights for American citizens at the outset of the Civil War without congressional authority. Here, it is Congress which has suspended habeas corpus rights—if they ever existed at all—for alien enemy combatants during wartime while our country remains under the threat of another terrorist invasion. Congress has that authority pursuant to the conditions spelled out in Article I, Section 9 of the Constitution. Congress is also granted the power to restrict the jurisdiction of the federal courts generally under Article III, Section 1. . . .

The Supreme Court should refuse to hear any appeal, since the President and Congress followed the Justices' instructions to the letter in removing the limits that Congress had placed on the President's authority. They took Justice Kennedy at his word when he said in his concurring opinion last year, "[B]ecause Congress has prescribed these limits, Congress can change them." President Bush went to Congress, and Congress changed the limits. In our constitutional republic, that should be the end of the story.

> "It is detrimental and unjust for a society to create an underclass of individuals with fewer rights or without the ability to exercise their human rights. ... undocumented immigrants should be granted full legal status."

Undocumented Workers Should Receive Legal Status

American Friends Service Committee

The American Friends Service Committee, founded in 1917 by the Society of Friends, also called the Quakers, carries out service, development, social justice, and peace programs throughout the world. In this viewpoint, the organization explains some of the terms used to refer to the provision of legal status to undocumented immigrants. The organization contends that under U.S. law and on a policy level, all undocumented immigrants should at least be provided with lawful permanent resident status to protect their human rights.

As you read, consider the following questions:

1. According to the American Friends Service Committee, what term was used in the Immigration Re-

American Friends Service Committee, "Legalization or Amnesty? Understanding the Debate," April 26, 2007. Reproduced by permission.

form and Control Act of 1986 that allowed undocumented immigrants to apply for permanent
residency?

2. What term under U.S. law, according to this viewpoint, is as of 2007 used to designate persons who
have the opportunity to apply for citizenship?

3. In the authors' view, what are some objections to
using the term "amnesty," when referring to granting a path to citizenship to undocumented immigrants?

Comprehensive immigration reform, legalization, amnesty,
earned adjustment, regularization, normalization—all of
these terms refer in some way to providing legal status to undocumented immigrants. They differ in their approach to *how*
immigrants should obtain legal status or for how long this legal status should last. Depending on who is using the terms,
they can refer to extremely different concepts.

Most people—immigrants, advocates, and policy makers—
refer to the measures adopted in 1986 as an "amnesty." The
Immigration Reform and Control Act of 1986 (IRCA) allowed
undocumented immigrants who had been living in the United
States since before January 1, 1982, to apply for permanent
residency.

Immigrant activists and other immigrants' rights advocates believe it is detrimental and unjust for a society to create
an underclass of individuals with fewer rights or without the
ability to exercise their human rights. Therefore, they believe
that undocumented immigrants should be granted full legal
status. Under current U.S. law, that is "lawful permanent resident" (LPR) status, which can later lead to the opportunity to
apply for citizenship. According to the most basic definition
above, what immigrants and advocates are pushing for is an
amnesty.

A Political Hot Potato

In the years since the passage of IRCA, the word "amnesty" has become a political hot potato—tossed around by proponents and opponents of the concept in order to label the other side. Immigrants and advocates who support amnesty are of two minds about the term "amnesty." Some say that "amnesty" means extending LPR status to undocumented immigrants; this is what happened in 1986, and it is what needs to happen again whether or not it includes other measures. In addition, it is a term that immigrant communities understand, especially the Spanish-speaking community with the translation "amnistia."

Within the immigrants' rights community, others argue that, although they also support granting LPR status to undocumented immigrants, legislators in Congress are unwilling to even begin a conversation if the term "amnesty" is used. Therefore, they prefer the term "legalization.". . .

A Difference in Terms

Some would also say that there is a substantive difference between the concepts of "legalization" and "amnesty," in that "legalization" would include a more stringent application process or other provisions, including measures to regulate future flows of migration. At the same time, however, others would argue that the concepts are exactly the same; the difference is simply the term.

Proponents of the term "legalization" argue that "amnesty" implies "forgiveness" for a "crime." Immigration, they believe, should not be seen as a crime. Proponents of the term "amnesty" say that no human being is illegal, and so they do not need to ask for "legalization." "Amnesty," they believe, is the more more appropriate term, because it asks forgiveness for breaking a law, albeit an unjust law. Amnesty International, for example, has been using the term for years, but it does not cast political prisoners in a negative light. And so, the debate continues.

Justice Requires It

Undocumented immigrants have the right to remain here and become an above-ground, legal part of our community.

Justice requires it.

Indeed, given the prior amnesty and citizenship granting in the 1980's, it would not be a stretch to say these present-day undocumented immigrants can reasonably expect to have the right to be put on a path to citizenship.

We owe them that.

And—could we be really honest about this—we owe them so much more.

Countless Americans have lived far more comfortable lives than they otherwise would have, because of these undocumented immigrants. . . .

We owe them our gratitude, we owe them our profound respect, and we owe them permanent residence and a path to citizenship.

Jack Clark,
"Undocumented Immigrants Have the Right to Stay Here,"
OPEDNEWS, May 5, 2006, www.opednews.com.

Amnesty Villified

Those who oppose providing legal status to undocumented immigrants have vilified the word "amnesty" so much that President Bush, in his January 7th statement on immigration reform, declared, "I oppose amnesty, placing undocumented workers on the automatic path to citizenship." It is important to note that President Bush implied yet another definition of "amnesty," which differs from those we have offered so far.

Members of Congress from both parties refrain from using the word "amnesty." Some use "legalization." Other terms are also used occasionally, including, "earned adjustment," "regularization," and "normalization." *Earned adjustment* tends to imply that the applicants for legal permanent resident status must "earn" their right to LPR status by promising to work additional years or fulfilling some other requirement besides having been an important member of the community for years. As a result, they may be granted some kind of "conditional" status before receiving LPR status. At times, *regularization* and *normalization* refer to granting temporary legal status, for example, through a guest worker program, rather than permanent residency. There have also been occasions, however, when these two terms have been used by policy makers as synonyms of legalization.

AFSC advocates for the full recognition and protection of the human rights of all people, including immigrants to the United States, documented or undocumented. Regardless of which term is used, AFSC affirms that, under U.S. laws and on a policy level, protecting the human rights of all requires, at the very least, providing LPR status to undocumented immigrants.

"Amnesties are the dark and sinister underbelly of our immigration process."

Undocumented Workers Should Not Receive Legal Status

Robert C. Byrd

In the following viewpoint, United States Senator Robert C. Byrd discusses the dangers of granting amnesty to illegal immigrants in the United States. He argues that there are millions of people waiting in line in their home countries to come into the U.S. illegally; those people should not be forced to wait even longer because others have chosen to flaunt the law. Byrd claims that rewarding those who break the law would serve to encourage more people to rush the borders and break the law. Robert C. Byrd is the Senator of West Virginia and is currently the longest-serving member in the history of the Senate.

As you read, consider the following questions:

1. If the Specter-Leahy Substitute were to be adopted, what does Senator Byrd claim it would do?

Robert C. Byrd, "Standing for Stronger Borders and Against Amnesty," April 4, 2006. http://byrd.senate.gov/speeches/2006_april/amnesty.html.

2. According to the Center for Immigration Studies, approximately how many immigrants are settling both legally and illegally in the United States each year?

3. Why does Senator Byrd claim that amnesties can be "dangerous, dangerous proposals"?

Today, I speak on the Specter-Leahy substitute to S. 2454, the Frist Border Security bill.

At the present time, the Frist bill contains no amnesty for illegal aliens. However, if the Specter-Leahy Substitute is adopted, it would effectively attach a massive amnesty for eight to twelve million illegal aliens. And provide those illegal aliens with a path to U.S. citizenship. According to immigration experts, the pending substitute amendment—with its guest-worker program, and amnesty for undocumented aliens—would open the gates to thirty million legal and illegal immigrants over the next decade.

I oppose this amnesty proposal—absolutely and unequivocally. I urge the Senate to pass a clean border security bill like the House did—without amnesty, without a guest-worker program, and without an increase in the annual allotment of permanent immigrant visas.

The U.S. "Remains Dangerously Exposed" To Terrorists

For more than four years, the nation has wondered how 19 terrorists managed to penetrate our border defenses to carry out the September 11 attacks. It chills the blood to think of those terrorists crossing our borders not once, but several times in the months before the attack—easily outsmarting our border security checks to plot their dastardly scheme. They walked among us as tourists, students, and business travelers. Three of them even stayed in the United States as illegal aliens.

Today, more than four years later, our country remains dangerously exposed to terrorists seeking to penetrate our border defenses. Since September 2001, an estimated two million new illegal immigrants have successfully beaten our border and interior security, and are now settled in the United States. That's two million new illegal immigrants since the Government pledged to regain control of the border after the 9/11 attacks.

Our immigration agencies are plagued with management and morale problems. They still do not have an exit-entry system with interoperable, biometric watch lists to accurately identify who is entering the country. We still cannot tell who is leaving the country. The requirement for foreign visitors to use biometric, machine-readable passports continues to be delayed, exempting millions of aliens each year from background checks. The Administration, still, stubbornly refuses to support the resources our border and interior enforcement agencies need to effectively do their jobs.

What Immigration Is Costing the U.S.

Meanwhile, the immigrant population continues to surge. The Center for Immigration Studies calculates that 1.5 million immigrants are settling both legally and illegally in the United States each year. The U.S. Census Bureau projects that immigration will be a major cause of the population of the United States increasing to 400 million people in less than 50 years.

The National Research Council estimates that the net fiscal cost of this massive immigration ranges from $11 billion to $22 billion per year, with the infrastructure of our nation—our schools, our health care system, our transportation and energy networks—increasingly unable to absorb this untenable surge in the population.

Many tout the additional border and interior enforcement personnel authorized since September 2001, but the president's budget has not come anywhere close to funding those authorizations. Homeland security expenditures have been capped at levels that prohibit the Congress from adequately filling the

U.S. Amnesties for Illegal Aliens

Until 1986, the United States had never forgiven the act of illegal immigration in other than individual cases and had never rewarded large numbers of illegal aliens with the opportunity for U.S. citizenship.

Congress has passed [several] amnesties for illegal aliens, starting in 1986.

1. Immigration and Reform Control Act (IRCA), 1986: *A blanket amnesty for some 2.7 million illegal aliens*

2. Section 245(i) Amnesty, 1994: *A temporary rolling amnesty for 578,000 illegal aliens*

3. Section 245(i) Extension Amnesty, 1997: *An extension of the rolling amnesty created in 1994*

4. Haitian Refugee Immigration Fairness Act Amnesty (HRIFA), 1998: *An amnesty for 125,000 illegal aliens from Haiti*

5. Late Amnesty, 2000: *An amnesty for some illegal aliens who claim they should have been amnestied under the 1986 IRCA amnesty, an estimated 400,000 illegal aliens*

"U.S. Amnesties for Illegal Aliens," NumbersUSA,
www.numbersusa.com/interests/amnesty.html.gaps.

Senator Gregg and I have had to fight for every additional nickle and dime that goes into our border security. It is never enough.

Immigration Enforcement Needs to Improve

Immigration enforcement in the United States remains decidedly, half-hearted. We are pulling our punches. Tougher border security mandates are signed into law, but then not fully funded. Statutory deadlines are set, but then indefinitely postponed. Undocumented aliens are denied Social Security cards, but then issued drivers licenses and taxpayer identification numbers. Employers are warned not to hire illegal labor, but then allowed to sponsor, without penalty, their illegal workforce for legal status. Funds are not requested to perform even the barest level of work site enforcement. We send troops abroad ostensibly so that we don't have to fight terrorists on American streets, but then we turn a blind-eye to millions of unauthorized, undocumented, unchecked aliens—any one of whom could be a potential terrorist.

When lawmakers and the so-called pundits comment that our current system is unworkable, it's because we haven't really tried to make it work. The contradictions in our immigration policies are undeniable. Lawmakers decry illegal immigration, but then advocate amnesty proposals which only encourages more illegal immigration. Advocates may try to distance themselves from that word—"amnesty". They may characterize their proposals as "guest-worker" programs or "temporary visas", but the effect is the same—to waive the rules for lawbreakers, and to legalize the unlawful actions of undocumented workers and the businesses that illegally employ them.

Amnesties Are Dangerous

Amnesties are the dark and sinister underbelly of our immigration process. They tarnish the magnanimous promise of a better life enshrined on the base of the Statue of Liberty. They minimize the struggle of all those who dutifully followed the rules to come to this country, and of all those who are still waiting abroad to immigrate legally. Amnesties undermine that great egalitarian and American principle that the law should apply equally and fairly to everyone. Amnesties perniciously decree that the law shall apply to some, but not to all.

Amnesties can be dangerous, dangerous proposals. Amnesties open routes to legal status for aliens hoping to circumvent the regular security checks. By allowing illegal aliens to adjust their status in the country, we allow them to bypass State Department checks normally done overseas through the visa and consular process. One need only look to the 1993 World Trade Center bombing, where one of the terrorist leaders had legalized his status through an amnesty, to clearly see the dangers of these kinds of proposals.

Our immigration system is already plagued with funding and staffing problems. It is overwhelmed on the borders, in the interior, and in its processing of immigration applications. It only took nineteen temporary visa holders to slip through the system to unleash the horror of the September 11 attacks. The pending proposal would shove 30 million legal and illegal aliens—many of whom have never gone through a background check—through our border security system, in effect, flooding a bureaucracy that is already drowning. It's a recipe for utter disaster.

Amnesties beget more illegal immigration—hurtful, destructive illegal immigration. They encourage other undocumented aliens to circumvent our immigration process in the hope that they too can achieve temporary worker status. Amnesties sanction the exploitation of illegal foreign labor by U.S. businesses, and encourage others businesses to hire cheap and illegal labor in order to compete.

President Reagan signed his amnesty proposal into law in 1986. At the time, I supported amnesty based on the same promises we hear today—that legalizing undocumented workers and increasing enforcement would stem the flow of illegal immigration. It didn't work then, and it won't work today. The 1986 amnesty failed miserably. After 1986, illegal immigrant population tripled from 2.7 million aliens, to 4 million aliens in 1996, to 8 million aliens in 2000, to an estimated 12 million illegal aliens today.

In that time, the Congress continued to enact amnesty after amnesty, waiving the Immigration Act for lawbreakers. The result is always the same—for every group of illegal aliens granted amnesty, a bigger group enters the country hoping to be similarly rewarded.

The Pending Amendment Is Flawed

The pending substitute amendment embodies this same flawed model. It's more of the same—more amnesties, more guest worker programs, more unfunded mandates on our immigration agencies. We ought to be focusing on how to limit the incentives for illegal immigration, and erase the contradictions in our immigration policies that encourage individuals on both sides of the border to flout the law and get away with it.

What's backwards about the pending substitute amendment is that it is actually rewarding illegal aliens. It rewards illegal behavior. It authorizes illegal aliens to work in the country. It grants illegal aliens a path to citizenship. It pardons employers who illegally employ unauthorized workers. It even repeals provisions in current law designed to deny cheaper, in-state tuition rates to illegal aliens.

The pending amendment is a big welcome mat for illegal immigrants. It is a misguided and dangerous proposal that would doom this Congress to the failures of previous Congresses.

The economist John Maynard Keynes once described the qualification for an economist as being the ability to study the present, in the light of the past, for the purpose of looking into the future. Patrick Henry echoed those sentiments more than a century earlier when he said "I have but one lamp by which my feet are guided, and that is the lamp of experience. I know of no way of judging the future but by the past."

Our nation's experience shows that amnesties do not work. They are dangerous proposals that reward and encourage illegal immigration. Our experience shows that we cannot play games with our border security or American lives could be lost.

I will oppose the Specter-Leahy substitute amendment, and I urge my colleagues to do likewise.

"For most defendants, the principal benefit of plea bargaining is receiving a lighter sentence for a less-severe charge than might result from taking the case to trial and losing."

Plea Bargains Expedite Justice

Grant D. Griffiths

Grant D. Griffiths is a Kansas criminal defense attorney and blogger. In this viewpoint, Griffiths discusses the benefits to criminal defendants of negotiating a plea agreement rather than taking the case to trial. Griffiths argues that a plea bargain provides both prosecution and defense attorneys with some control over the result of the case while moving it quickly through the court system.

As you read, consider the following questions:

1. In Griffiths's opinion, what is the principal benefit of plea bargaining for most defendants?
2. What are some benefits, according to Griffiths, of getting a charge reduced from a felony to a misdemeanor as a result of a plea bargain?

Grant D. Griffiths, "Defendants' Incentives for Accepting Plea Bargains," Kansas Criminal Defense Attorney Blog, http://gdgrifflaw.typepad.com, October 24, 2005. Copyright © 2005 NOLO. Reproduced by permission.

3. Griffiths contends that some famous defendants may enter into a plea bargain to avoid publicity. In what ways does the author argue this would help keep their names out of the public eye?

A s criminal courts become more crowded, prosecutors and judges feel increased pressure to move cases quickly through the system. Trials can take days, weeks or sometimes months, while guilty pleas can often be arranged in minutes. Also, the outcome of any given trial is usually unpredictable—but a plea bargain provides both prosecution and defense with some control over the result.

For most defendants, the principal benefit of plea bargaining is receiving a lighter sentence for a less-severe charge than might result from taking the case to trial and losing. In addition, defendants who are represented by private counsel can save a bundle on attorney fees by accepting a plea bargain. It almost always takes more time and effort to bring a case to trial than to negotiate and handle a plea bargain.

There are other benefits as well:

Benefits of a Plea Bargain

Getting out of jail. Defendants who are held in custody—who either do not have the right to bail or cannot afford bail, or who do not qualify for release on their own recognizance—may get out of jail immediately following the judge's acceptance of a plea. Depending on the offense, the defendant may get out altogether, on probation, with or without some community service obligations. Or, the defendant may have to serve more time but will still get out much sooner than if he or she insisted on going to trial.

Resolving the matter quickly. This has the intangible benefit, touched on above, of providing resolution to the stress of being charged with a crime. Going to trial usually requires a much longer wait—and causes much more stress—than taking a plea bargain.

Plea Bargains Waive Rights, Save Time

Plea bargaining can conclude a criminal case without a trial. When it is successful, plea bargaining results in a plea agreement between the prosecutor and defendant. In this agreement the defendant agrees to plead guilty without a trial, and in return the prosecutor agrees to dismiss certain charges or make favorable sentence recommendations to the court. Plea bargaining is expressly authorized in statutes and in court rules. . . .

Generally, a judge will authorize a plea bargain if the defendant makes a knowing and voluntary waiver of his or her right to a trial, the defendant understands the charges, the defendant understands the maximum sentence he or she could receive after pleading guilty, and the defendant makes a voluntary confession, in court, to the alleged crime. Even if a defendant agrees to plead guilty, a judge may decline to accept the guilty plea and plea agreement if the charge or charges have no factual basis.

The judge does not participate in plea bargain discussions. Prosecutors have discretion whether to offer a plea bargain. However, a prosecutor may not base the determination of whether to negotiate on the basis of an unjustifiable standard such as race, religion, or some other arbitrary classification.

Plea bargaining can be advantageous for both prosecutors and defendants. Prosecutors may seek a plea bargain in certain cases to save valuable court time for high-priority cases. Prosecutors often are amenable to plea bargaining with a defendant who admits guilt and accepts responsibility for a crime: plea bargaining in this context is considered the defendant's reward for confessing. . . .

"Plea Bargain," West's Encyclopedia of American Law,
The Gale Group Inc., 1998.

Having fewer or less-serious offenses on one's record. Pleading guilty or no contest in exchange for a reduction in the number of charges or the seriousness of the offenses looks a lot better on a defendant's record than the convictions that might result following a trial. This can be particularly important if the defendant is ever convicted in the future. For example, a second conviction for driving under the influence (DUI) may carry mandatory jail time, whereas if the first DUI offense had been bargained down to reckless driving, there may be no jail time for the "second" DUI.

Sentence Reduction

Even for people who are never rearrested, getting a charge reduced from a felony to a misdemeanor, or from a felony that constitutes a strike under a "three strikes" law to one that doesn't, can prove to be a critical benefit. Some professional licenses must be forfeited upon conviction of a felony. Future employers may not want to hire someone previously convicted of a felony. Felony convictions may be used in certain court proceedings (even civil cases) to discredit people who testify as witnesses. Felons can't own or possess firearms. And, in many jurisdictions, felons can't vote.

Having a less socially stigmatizing offense on one's record. Prosecutors may reduce charges that are perceived as socially offensive to less-offensive charges in exchange for a guilty plea. For example, a prosecutor may reduce a molestation or rape case to an assault. This can have a major impact on the defendant's relationship with friends and family. Perhaps even more critical, sometimes defendants convicted of stigmatizing offenses may be at a greater risk of being harmed (or killed) in prison than if they are convicted of an offense that doesn't carry the same stigma.

Avoiding hassles. Some people plead guilty—especially to routine, minor first offenses—without hiring a lawyer. If they waited to go to trial, they would have to find a good lawyer and spend both time and money preparing for trial.

Avoiding publicity. Famous people, ordinary people who depend on their reputation in the community to earn a living, and people who don't want to bring further embarrassment to their families all may chose to plead guilty or no contest to keep their names out of the public eye. While news of the plea itself may be public, the news is short-lived compared to news of a trial. And rarely is a defendant's background explored in the course of a plea bargain to the extent it may be done at trial.

Keeping others out of the case. Some defendants plead guilty to take the blame (sometimes called the "rap") for someone else, or to end the case quickly so that others who may be jointly responsible are not investigated.

"*Given the Fifth Amendment's prohibition of compelled self-incrimination and the Sixth Amendment's guarantee of impartial juries, one would think that the administration of criminal justice in America would be marked by adversarial trials—and yet, the opposite is true. Fewer than 10 percent of the criminal cases brought by the federal government each year are actually tried before juries with all of the accompanying procedural safeguards . . ."*

Plea Bargains Jeopardize Justice

Timothy Lynch

Timothy Lynch is an attorney and the director of the Cato Institute's Project on Criminal Justice. He is the editor of After Prohibition: An Adult Approach to Drug Policies in the 21st Century. *In this viewpoint, Lynch argues for the abolishment of the practice of plea bargaining. He contends that plea bargaining is unconstitutional and a deliberate technique used by the government to bypass the institutional safeguards in trials.*

Timothy Lynch, "The Case Against Plea Bargaining," *Regulation*, fall 2003, pp. 24–27.

As you read, consider the following questions:

1. In the author's view, what safeguards to the accused are explicitly guaranteed in the Bill of Rights?

2. When the prosecutor offers a plea bargain deal to a defendant, promising a reduced prison sentence, what rights does the defendant waive?

3. Which Supreme Court case sanctioned the practice of plea bargaining? In your opinion, is the fact that plea bargaining speeds caseload disposition enough of a justification for the practice?

Plea bargaining has come to dominate the administration of justice in America. According to one legal scholar, "Every two seconds during a typical workday, a criminal case is disposed of in an American courtroom by way of a guilty plea or nolo contendere plea."

Even though plea bargaining pervades the justice system, I argue that the practice should be abolished because it is unconstitutional.

The Rise and Fall of Adversarial Trials

Because any person who is accused of violating the criminal law can lose his liberty, and perhaps even his life depending on the offense and prescribed penalty, the Framers of the Constitution took pains to put explicit limits on the awesome powers of government. The Bill of Rights explicitly guarantees several safeguards to the accused, including the right to be informed of the charges, the right not to be compelled to incriminate oneself, the right to a speedy and public trial, the right to an impartial jury trial in the state and district where the offense allegedly took place, the right to cross-examine the state's witnesses, the right to call witnesses on one's own behalf, and the right to the assistance of counsel.

Justice Hugo Black once noted that, in America, the defendant "has an absolute, unqualified right to compel the State to investigate its own case, find its own witnesses, prove its own facts, and convince the jury through its own resources. Throughout the process, the defendant has a fundamental right to remain silent, in effect challenging the State at every point to 'Prove it!'" By limiting the powers of the police and prosecutors, the Bill of Rights safeguards freedom.

Given the Fifth Amendment's prohibition of compelled self-incrimination and the Sixth Amendment's guarantee of impartial juries, one would think that the administration of criminal justice in America would be marked by adversarial trials—and yet, the opposite is true. Fewer than 10 percent of the criminal cases brought by the federal government each year are actually tried before juries with all of the accompanying procedural safeguards noted above. More than 90 percent of the criminal cases in America are never tried, much less proven, to juries. The overwhelming majority of individuals who are accused of crime forgo their constitutional rights and plead guilty.

The rarity of jury trials is not the result of criminals who come into court to relieve a guilty conscience or save taxpayers the costs of a trial. The truth is that government officials have deliberately engineered the system to assure that the jury trial system established by the Constitution is seldom used. And plea bargaining is the primary technique used by the government to bypass the institutional safeguards in trials.

Plea bargaining consists of an agreement (formal or informal) between the defendant and the prosecutor. The prosecutor typically agrees to a reduced prison sentence in return for the defendant's waiver of his constitutional right against self-incrimination and his right to trial. As one critic has written, "The leniency is payment to a defendant to induce him or her not to go to trial. The guilty plea or no contest plea is the quid pro quo for the concession; there is no other reason."

"Signing Away Their Lives"

In the United States, more than 90 percent of all cases in the justice system are settled by plea bargaining rather than exercising the right to trial. The rate of felony convictions of nonviolent crimes in communities of color is overwhelming: African Americans constitute 13 percent of all drug users, yet they represent 35 percent of arrests, 55 percent of convictions and 74 percent of prison sentences, according to a 2000 study by the Sentencing Project.

These two factors mean that the widespread practice of plea bargaining—where prosecutors overcharge for a crime and defense attorneys usually urge defendants to cop a plea for a lighter sentence—has increased repercussions for people of color who end up literally signing away their lives on the dotted line. Defendants are seldom informed about the underlying effects of pleading to a felony—such a losing their right to vote, access to federal student aid, and if they are noncitizens, being deported.

Rolanda J. West, "What a Bargain: The Widespread Practice of Plea Bargaining Has Increased Repercussions for People of Color who End Up Literally Signing Away Their Lives on the Dotted Line," Colorlines Magazine, *vol. 7, no. 3, fall 2004.*

Plea bargaining unquestionably alleviates the workload of judges, prosecutors, and defense lawyers. But is it proper for a government that is constitutionally required to respect the right to trial by jury to use its charging and sentencing powers to pressure an individual to waive that right? There is no doubt that government officials deliberately use their power to pressure people who have been accused of crime, and who are presumed innocent, to confess their guilt and waive their right to a formal trial. We know this to be true because prosecutors freely admit that this is what they do. . . .

Government Retaliation?

Plea bargaining rests on the constitutional fiction that our government does not retaliate against individuals who wish to exercise their right to trial by jury. Although the fictional nature of that proposition has been apparent to many for some time now, what is new is that more and more people are reaching the conclusion that it is intolerable. Chief Judge William G. Young of the Federal District Court in Massachusetts, for example, recently filed an opinion that was refreshingly candid about what is happening in the modern criminal justice system:

> Evidence of sentencing disparity visited on those who exercise their Sixth Amendment right to trial by jury is today stark, brutal, and incontrovertible. . . . Today, under the Sentencing Guidelines regime with its vast shift of power to the Executive, that disparity has widened to an incredible 500 percent. As a practical matter this means, as between two similarly situated defendants, that if the one who pleads and cooperates gets a four-year sentence, then the guideline sentence for the one who exercises his right to trial by jury and is convicted will be 20 years. Not surprisingly, such a disparity imposes an extraordinary burden on the free exercise of the right to an adjudication of guilt by one's peers. Criminal trial rates in the United States and in this District are plummeting due to the simple fact that today we punish people—punish them severely—simply for going to trial. It is the sheerest sophistry to pretend otherwise. . . .

Unconstitutional Speed

Thomas Jefferson famously observed that "the natural progress of things is for liberty to yield and government to gain ground." The American experience with plea bargaining is yet another confirmation of that truth. The Supreme Court unleashed a runaway train when it sanctioned plea bargaining in *Bordenkircher v. Hayes*. Despite a steady media diet of titillating criminal trials in recent years, there is an increasing recognition that jury trials are now a rarity in America—and that something, somewhere, is seriously amiss. That "something" is plea bargaining.

As with so many other areas of constitutional law, the Court must stop tinkering around the edges of the issue and return to first principles. It is true that plea bargaining speeds caseload disposition, but it does so in an unconstitutional manner. The Framers of the Constitution were aware of less time-consuming trial procedures when they wrote the Bill of Rights, but chose not to adopt them. The Framers believed the Bill of Rights, and the freedom it secured, was well worth any costs that resulted. If that vision is to endure, the Supreme Court must come to its defense.

Periodical Bibliography

The following articles have been selected to supplement the diverse views presented in this chapter.

Mike Cutler	"U.S. Citizenship & Immigration Services Refuses to Learn at Our Peril," *The Family Security Foundation*, December 6, 2006, www.familysecuritymatters.org.
Aaron Glantz	"Military Plea Bargains Raise Questions of Justice," *One World*, November 19, 2006, www.worldproutassembly.org.
Alberto R. Gonzales	"Opposing View: They lost my confidence—Attorneys' dismissals were related to performance, not to politics," *USA Today*, March 7, 2007, www.usatoday.com.
Alfredo Gutierrez	"The Sins of the Fathers: The Children of Undocumented Immigrants Pay the Price," *Perspectives on Immigration*, American Immigration Law Foundation, January 26, 2007, www.ailf.org.
Ruben Navarrette	"Gonzales Should Stay," *Real Clear Politics*, March 22, 2007, www.realclearpolitics.com.
Keith Olbermann	"The Death of Habeas Corpus," *Countdown*, October 10, 2006, www.countdown.msnbc.com.
James Ridgeway	"Attention Immigrants: Thanks for Your Hard Work. Now Leave," *Mother Jones*, May 26, 2007, www.commondreams.org.
Matthew Robinson	"Freedom in an Era of Terror: A Critical Analysis of the USA Patriot Act," *Justice Policy Journal*, vol. 4, no. 1, Spring 2007.
Shankar Vedantam	"Out of Unenforceable Laws, Amnesties Are Born," *Washington Post*, June 4, 2007.

OPPOSING
VIEWPOINTS®
SERIES

CHAPTER 4

What Should Be the Role of the Media in the Legal System?

Chapter Preface

In the U.S. legal system, the accused has the right to a public trial. Presiding judges, charged with ensuring the rights of all parties involved in a legal dispute, must balance the right to a public trial with their responsibility to maintain order and decorum in the courtroom. Media access, particularly in high-profile trials, has been an ongoing source of concern and debate.

Most states allow some level of access to cameras inside the courtroom as set forth in the Rules of Court for each state. Judges in some jurisdictions retain the sole discretion to ban cameras from the courtroom. Rule 30 of the Tennessee State Supreme Court outlines criteria a judge might properly invoke to justify a prohibition of courtroom cameras. These circumstances are: "to keep order and prevent distractions; to ensure the safety of any party, witness, or juror; or to ensure a fair trial."

Media-access advocate Barbara Cochran, president of Radio-Television News Directors Association and Foundation, contends that some of the measures that restrict media access to the courtrooms may "compromise the right of the public to observe the judicial process." In her view, "banning cameras from the courtroom means the most accurate account of what transpired in a trial will not be available to the public."

Limits on media access must be appropriate to meet the ends of justice. Yet competing media sources, and new forms of mass media, including courtroom bloggers posting live reports, have raised additional issues of what constitutes appropriate access in the public interest. The Constitution protects both the right to a fair trial and freedom of speech and of the press. Some legal scholars and courtroom lawyers are concerned that intense media coverage may bring both of these fundamental rights into direct conflict.

A doctrine of the U.S. legal system holds that all criminal defendants are presumed innocent until a prosecutor proves guilt beyond a reasonable doubt. However, Mark J. Geragos, writing in 2007 in the *Loyola of Los Angeles Law Review*, contends that "extensive media coverage can render the presumption of innocence meaningless." Geragos, who served as defense attorney in the high-profile cases of both Susan McDougal and Scott Peterson, argues that "Objective reporting has given way to a new journalism—a subjective form of fact-telling known to participants as 'advocacy journalism'—which blurs the line between fact and opinion. It seems that this erosion in objectivity has led reporters to take a position, to either praise or bash, because confrontation is what sells. And I believe it is this subservience to commercial objectives which has skewed the free press, fair trial calculus."

The Reporters Committee for Freedom of the Press, a media-access advocacy group and publisher of *Secret Justice*, a series of reports on access to the judicial system, argues "the media, as the public's representative, needs to be aware of threats to openness in court proceedings, and must be prepared to fight to ensure continued access to trials."

In chapter 4, various authors present their views on the relationship between the media and the judicial process. Questions about who are considered legitimate media and what forms of mass communication should be given courtroom access will continue to be debated. The role of media in the workings of the U.S. legal system will likely be a source of ongoing tension in the struggle to find a just balance between competing rights.

> "...[B]logs can help undercut the sad
> but all too true observation of journal-
> ist A.J. Liebling: 'Freedom of the press
> is guaranteed only to those who own
> one.'"

Internet Bloggers Should Have Media Access to Courtrooms

A Progressive on the Prairie

A Progressive on the Prairie is an Internet blog written by an attorney in Sioux Falls, South Dakota, who formerly worked as a newspaper and UPI wire service reporter covering the South Dakota Supreme Court and state and federal trial courts. In this viewpoint, the author contends that bloggers need no special credentials to cover court proceedings. He argues that one of the best things about blogs is that they allow almost anyone a low-cost means of distributing ideas, analysis, and criticism worldwide.

As you read, consider the following questions:

1. In the author's report, of the one hundred media seats at the 2007 Scooter Libby trial, how many

A Progressive on the Prairie, "Credentialing Bloggers," January 12, 2007. Reproduced by permission.

were set aside for Internet bloggers? What association does the author credit with obtaining these media seats for bloggers?

2. The author contends that attendance at trials in state or federal court in South Dakota would pose no problem for bloggers. In the author's opinion does the press have a greater right of access to court proceedings than the public?

3. What problems does the author cite in his argument against the credentialing of bloggers as proposed by the Media Bloggers Association? In your view, would credentialing bloggers ensure that they adhere to certain ethical standards?

I saw today via BoingBoing that an outfit known as the Media Bloggers Association (MBA) obtained two seats for bloggers out of the 100 set aside for the media in what will certainly be an overflowing courtroom for the the trial of Scooter Libby, Vice President Cheney's former chief of staff. Here's what the [*Washington Post*] reported, including its traditional press shot at bloggers:

> The common journalistic practices of verifying facts, seeking both sides of a story and subjecting an article to editing are honored mostly in the breach. Innuendo and rumor ricochet around the Internet as blogs link from one to another, at times making defamatory voices indistinguishable from the many others involved in this experiment of free expression.
>
> Yet, after detailed talks with [MBA's president], officials at the U.S. District Court decided that public awareness of court proceedings could be enhanced by his group's members, among them documentary filmmaker and journalist Rory O'Connor (www.roryoconnor.org/blog) and freelance writer James Joyner (www.outsidethebeltway.com).

"Bloggers can bring a depth of reporting that some traditional media organizations aren't able to achieve because of space and time limitations," said Sheldon Snook, administrative assistant to Chief Judge Thomas F. Hogan. Snook added that some bloggers also bring expertise that is welcome in court.

I think Snook's assessment is very accurate. For example, when I covered the South Dakota Supreme Court while working for UPI and the state and federal trial courts in Rapid City, most of my knowledge came from *The Reporter and the Law* by Lyle Denniston, the *Baltimore Sun* reporter who has covered the U.S. Supreme Court for decades. While Denniston's book is a superb resource for anyone wanting to understand the workings of the justice system, blawgers (law bloggers) undoubtedly can provide insight and expertise that non-lawyer reporters cannot.

At the same time, in 99.9 percent of all trials in state or federal court in South Dakota, attendance would pose no problem for bloggers. They would simply go and sit down like any other member of the public (although "live blogging" or using a laptop in the courtroom might face some restrictions depending on noise levels or concern that material not presented at trial might get displayed on the laptop). After all, press rights of access to court proceedings are no greater or less than the public's.

While MBA should probably be commended for its efforts, part of the [*Washington Post*] story, if accurate, disturbs me. It says MBA's president wants to help create "an elite tier of bloggers." Admittance to this group would result from being credentialed by the MBA after agreeing to adhere to its ethical standards and, thereby, "win them access to news and sporting events, advance copies of new books for review and entrance to advance screening of moves." There are two problems with this concept.

No Marble Walls in Cyberspace

The Internet has utterly collapsed the notion of a "news cycle," and stories run as they happen. The change in the intervening years at the Court has been rather remarkable. Not only do bloggers now post their accounts of oral argument within two to three hours of leaving the courtroom, but even the traditional print journalists now scramble to post online editions of their stories that same afternoon.

As the time frame for producing news has shortened, the community of online "reporters" has expanded. Whereas Americans once had to rely exclusively on the print, radio, and TV "experts" for an account of the day's events, the Web has made it possible for visiting law students, lawyers, and even the parties to the dispute to post their impressions of oral argument almost instantaneously. . . .

In an article in the *Washington Post*, Michael Kinsley made another important observation about bloggers: They create a fundamentally democratic community of shared interests, in which there are no rules dictating page length, credentials of writers, or which letters to the editor might make the cut. As a consequence, the Web has fostered more than just a cacophony of new voices to report on the doings of the Supreme Court; it's opened up a dialogue between far-flung experts. Law professors in California immediately correct misimpressions in New Jersey, and attorneys in Boston challenge constitutional analysis coming out of Seattle. The public no longer listens passively to the events of day.

Dahlia Lithwick, "High Court Ethereality,"
The American Lawyer, *February 1, 2005.*

First much of this happens already without the MBA or any other organization being a credentialing entity. Bloggers attended and covered the national political conventions two years ago. I guarantee bloggers get plenty of press releases and invitations to events from various campaigns and organizations, just like the traditional media. I know of at least one podcaster unaffiliated with any traditional media outlet who is considered part of the authorized media for a minor league hockey team in a large metropolitan area. Blogcritics, to which I contribute, is one of several sites through which bloggers receive advance copies of books, CDs and DVDs and are invited to advance screenings. In fact, there's dozens of "litblogs" out there the publishing industry recognizes as providing coverage of books and publishing matters. It is not uncommon for me to receive ARCs (advance reading copies) from a variety of national publishing houses.

Second and perhaps more important, I look askance at any effort to proclaim one segment of a group of similarly situated individuals as the "elite," who are thereby entitled to advantages over the others. Designating an "elite tier" of bloggers strikes me as particularly contrary to one of the best things about blogs—they allow almost anyone a low-cost means of distributing ideas, analysis and criticism worldwide. As such, blogs can help undercut the sad but all too true observation of journalist A.J. Liebling: "Freedom of the press is guaranteed only to those who own one."

Undoubtedly, adhering to certain ethical standards behooves bloggers and their readers. But it isn't just "this experiment of free expression" that is guilty of ethical lapses. Likewise, just how good a job did the [*Washington Post*] and the rest of the traditional press do "verifying facts [and] seeking both sides of a story" in the run up to the Iraq War? That's part of the reason why an "elite" stamp from any particular organization should never become the determinant of the legitimacy of any individual or collective blog.

> *"Today owning a press takes no more than a visit to a cybercafe or the local public library. And that's an empowering change. But it's not an unadulterated good. By tossing out the old restrictions on disseminating news, we are also giving up some important protections."*

Internet Bloggers Should Not Have Media Access to the Courtroom

James McGrath Morris

James McGrath Morris is a Washington, DC, author who writes about American journalism history. As of 2007, he was at work on a biography of nineteenth-century publishing magnate Joseph Pulitzer, whose Pulitzer Prize is awarded for excellence in journalism and other literary areas. In this viewpoint, Morris discusses the admission of Internet bloggers to the courtroom press pool to cover the Scooter Libby trial. He provides historical context to argue that while the technology is new, what bloggers are doing often is not. "This newfangled form of journalism," in Morris' view, may not necessarily be such a wonderful thing for democracy.

James McGrath Morris, "Commentary: Bloggers' Big News Needs Scaling Down," *Legal Times*, February 28, 2007. www.law.com. Reproduced by permission.

As you read, consider the following questions:

1. The author gives an historical account of a trial that drew so much competing media that journalists devised unique systems to provide the "freshest copy in town." In Morris' opinion, what is the danger when media bloggers focus on "lightning speed?"

2. According to Morris, media bloggers admit to the inclusion of personal opinion into their reporting. Is this a new concept in reporting news, according to Morris?

3. The author contends that "everyone needs an editor," and questions how the public or truth is served when serious errors occur. What is one of the purposes of a professional news media, according to the author?

As they come, this judicial first wasn't exactly front-page news—that is, if you are still in the habit of reading a quaint, old-fashioned newspaper. But in cyberspace the decision of the U.S. District Court to include bloggers as bona fide members of the press pool during the recent "Scooter" Libby trial was big news. For the first time ever in a federal court case, bloggers were officially welcomed as equals with newspaper and broadcast reporters, albeit in a little room down the hall from the actual trial in Courtroom 16.

It took the Media Bloggers Association two years of negotiations with court officials to win the right to join the media frenzy. Kim Pearson, a professor at the College of New Jersey, was among the vanguard who took a turn in the press pool. According to Pearson, Judge Reggie Walton's decision to allow bloggers to participate in the trial opened "a new chapter in the debate over the legitimacy of bloggers as gatherers and disseminators of news."

True. But it may not be a debate favorable to blogging. The admission of bloggers into a press pool serves as a timely moment to examine the Achilles' heel of this newfangled form of journalism. Despite all its claims of whiz-bang newness and democracy-promoting attributes, blogging may turn out to be nothing more than a fresh version of an old journalistic gimmick. More important, it may not necessarily be such a wonderful thing for democracy.

Hot Off the Presses

First, while the technology is new, what bloggers are doing often isn't. Reporting the latest from a courtroom at lightning speed is an old pursuit.

Exactly a century ago, Irvin Cobb, a star reporter for Joseph Pulitzer's *New York Evening World*, was assigned to cover what was called the "Trial of the Century" (until O.J. Simpson walked into a California courtroom 87 years later). Harry K. Thaw was facing murder charges for having shot architect Stanford White at Madison Square Garden in a dispute over the affections of Evelyn Nesbit, a chorus girl of great beauty. The media attention was unlike any that America had seen before, and the crush of reporters and lawyers left no room for the general public. Telegraph cables poured down into the courthouse through its central skylight, and Western Union opened an office in the main hall. William Randolph Hearst assigned three women to cover the trial for the *New York Journal*. The court, unused to women, set up a special table for them in the front of the room.

Cobb and his city editor, the infamous Charles Chapin, devised a system to beat the competition. Two copy boys were assigned to stand behind Cobb. One kept him supplied with freshly sharpened pencils. The other grabbed each completed sheet of Cobb's copy and ran it downstairs to a basement corridor, where another reporter, Johnny Gavin, read it over a private telephone line to a stenographer in the *Evening World* city room.

No more than a few minutes passed before Cobb's words went into type, giving his paper the freshest copy in town for its hourly editions eagerly hawked by newsboys on the streets of Manhattan. Soon readers were hooked on Cobb's voluminous daily accounts—a pre-cyberspace blog, if you wish—sometimes exceeding 12,000 words.

Cobb's tale is a reminder that the "wow" factor is so strong that it sometimes blinds bloggers and their advocates to the danger inherent in our love of technology's new capabilities. By focusing on the lightning speed of unfettered Internet communication, bloggers are in danger of fulfilling Marshall McLuhan's nightmare that the medium would become the message. In the end, content matters. All the high-tech bells and whistles should not distract us from that.

Beware, He's Got an Opinion

Bloggers are quick to claim that they bring something new to the public debate because they are untrained (read untainted) citizen journalists. That, however, is hardly a novelty in media history. Journalism schools, which are only a century old, have not yet become a required prerequisite to being a reporter. In fact, until a few years ago, not going to a journalism school was considered a badge of some merit in many media circles. Compared to lawyers and accountants, journalists can hardly claim professional training.

Additionally, bloggers play up the fact that they mix in their opinions with their reporting. Bloggers challenge "the theory of objective journalism," Robert Cox, president of the Media Bloggers Association, told the *New York Times*. "They're putting in a lot more opinion and lot more color than the traditional reporters."

A visit to any newspaper archive would prove that this advance is no more than a retreat to the golden age of newspapers, when reporters piled their copy high with inflammatory adjectives, personal conclusions and conjectures as facts. Take, for instance, the *Chicago Tribune*'s front-page reporting on an accused murderer sought by the police: "The blood-stained monster who crushed out their breath of life is free, with nothing to prevent him from committing another heinous crime." After his capture, on the eve of his trial, the paper headlined its story, "Thou Art the Man!"

The drive for objectivity is a modern journalism concept. While many may welcome the reintroduction of personal opinion into reporting, it can hardly be called a new approach.

To their credit, the men and women who wield the pencils—oops, laptops—of today are doing something different. But it's not the technology or the lack of training or even the re-introduction of opinion into the news; it's the dissemination of their work that makes blogging a new phase in journalism history.

To be a blogger, one needs only access to a computer and a few dollars to pay for a Web site, and even the latter isn't strictly necessary as some sites offer free blogging space. "By empowering individual writers, by reducing the costs of entry into publishing to close to zero, the blog revolution has only begun to transform the media world," Andrew Sullivan heralded in an oft-quoted 2002 article in the *Sunday Times of London*, considered almost a manifesto of the blogosphere.

In the old days, media critic A.J. Liebling quipped that "freedom of the press belongs to a man who owns one." Today owning a press takes no more than a visit to a cybercafe or the local public library. And that's an empowering change.

But it's not an unadulterated good. By tossing out the old restrictions on disseminating news, we are also giving up some important protections.

A Second Pair of Eyes

Everyone needs an editor. Good writing is a collaborative process in which the give-and-take strengthens the final product. This article, for instance, had its genesis in a lengthy e-mail. Then it morphed into a draft of an article that was reviewed by an editor, who found problems, weak points and maybe potential mistakes. The final version, which you are now reading, was edited further [note to editor: should that be farther?].

If journalism is the first draft of history, unedited blogs are more like the first draft of journalism. This may make the copy fresh and exciting, and if it includes a few typos, so what? The socialite who is called a socialist will recover from the insult.

But what happens when the error is more serious, such as the case of the blogger who erroneously reported that an employee died because the corporation blocked 911 calls on its phone system? How is the public or the truth served then?

"Blog posting errors are rarely discussed in blogging circles. They are a bit of a dirty little secret, you might say," Wayne Hurlbert, a Canadian blogger with a penchant for honesty, admits. His suggestion? "The best idea, of course, is to always proofread your posts before clicking the Publish button."

This still presumes that writers are their own best editors. Not only is this false, but it discounts the important public function of editors. One of the purposes of a professional news media is to act as a gatekeeper for actual facts and honest debate. Blogging, which revolves almost entirely around individuals rather than institutions, leaves readers with a bewildering array of unattributed sources of information.

Granted, the gatekeepers do stumble, such as when the press chose to hide President Franklin Roosevelt's failing health from the public. But the mainstream media has built a track record of reliability, and the public recognizes that. It is with good reason most of us are more likely to trust a report in the *Washington Post* than the latest scoop in the *National Enquirer*.

A Simple Case of Overkill

Moreover, blogging may be more democratic, but it's also likely to be less read. There is a point when there are simply too many blogs. With 30 millions blogs today, we may well have reached that point.

"That's a lot of reading," said David Weinberger, a fellow at Harvard University's Berkman Center on Internet and Society, who announced on National Public Radio that he would no longer be reading many of his friends' blogs. Who has the time? "A salad bar that is five miles long is as useless to me as one that is 3,000 miles long because I am getting all the salad I can eat in the first 15 feet," Weinberger said.

Blogging furthers the ongoing fragmentation of the media. Families used to gather at evening time around the television to watch Walter Cronkite deliver the news. Today, cable and satellite offer dozens of alternatives. When Knopf brought out an unknown author such as Thomas Wolfe, readers across the nation rushed to the bookstore. Today, with a proliferation of publishers bringing out more than 175,000 titles a year, who would know if there were another Wolfe in the mix? Gone too are the general-interest magazines like *Look* and *Life*.

When we gather at the office water cooler to talk, it is becoming increasingly unlikely that any two of us will have seen the same TV program, read the same book or shared the same news account of an event. With the profusion of cell-phone photojournalism, we may not even have seen the same pictures.

If blogging is the way of the future, then instead of a public who collectively shares major events, there will be hundreds, if not thousands, of smaller, isolated groups gaining vastly different takes on the day's news. In the end, we may all

175

be reading our own words. As beauty lies in the eyes of the beholder, blogging's fate rests in the eyes of readers. If it's a mirror into which we stare all day, we'll be in trouble.

> "The move to introduce cameras into the Supreme Court's super secret courtroom is not new. Nor are the many objections that have been raised against it. Since the decision about allowing cameras is solely left up to the justices, it's probably not surprising that cameras are still barred from the high court—even though all 50 states and other federal courts have at least experimented with them, often with great success."

Cameras Should Be Allowed in the U.S. Supreme Court

Dahlia Lithwick

Dahlia Lithwick is a senior editor and Supreme Court correspondent for Slate, *an online magazine of news and commentary on culture and politics. In this viewpoint, Lithwick proposes that U.S. Supreme Court oral arguments—the "job performance" aspect—be televised, while blacking out the confirmation hearings for appointing justices—the "job interviews." The author dis-*

Dahlia Lithwick, "Justice Showtime: Supreme Court Justices Have Long Worked Behind a Secret Veil. But Televising Their Arguments Would Serve Democracy Well," *American Lawyer*, vol. 27, no. 12, December 2005, pp. 130–31. Copyright © 2005 American Lawyer Media L.P. Reproduced by permission.

cusses some of the objections to televising oral arguments, a change she contends will increase public approval of the Court.

As you read, consider the following questions:

1. The author mentions several counterarguments to allowing cameras into the oral argument phase of U.S. Supreme Court proceedings. What are some of these objections?

2. Which objection, according to the author, is the real reason the Supreme Court justices do not allow televised sessions?

3. In what ways, in the author's opinion, would television in the Supreme Court serve democracy?

If you want to learn about a U.S. Supreme Court justice's ideology and preferences, Senate confirmation hearings are about as useful as consultations with a Magic 8-Ball. Anyone forced to suffer through hour upon hour of senatorial speechifying knows that whatever the purpose of these exercises is, it's most assuredly not to glean any understanding of the nominee's views. Indeed, there is no tool on earth that is going to reveal a justice's views, including polygraph, x-ray, or torture, due to the First Rule of Confirmations: Thou Shalt Have No Opinions in the First Place.

As hideous as these proceedings may be, they are made even worse by the omnipresent television cameras. Cameras create all the wrong incentives for the committee members: to speak rather than listen; to look smart rather than be smart; and to sink a solid three-point sound bite rather than ferret out truthful testimony. And here's the real irony: We televise confirmation hearings, but don't televise Supreme Court oral arguments. So at the end of the day, the American public gets to sit in on the job interview, but the job performance is blacked out.

Here, then, is my modest proposal: Let's switch things around and televise Supreme Court oral arguments while blacking out the confirmation hearings. That way, the senators will have less incentive to act up and act out, while the justices will have more incentive to behave like philosopher kings.

The move to introduce cameras into the Supreme Court's supersecret courtroom is not new. Nor are the many objections that have been raised against it. Since the decision about allowing cameras is solely left up to the justices, it's probably not surprising that cameras are still barred from the high court—even though all 50 states and other federal courts have at least experimented with them, often with great success. The main counterarguments have to do with the purity of the proceedings: Cameras would be used to distort and mischaracterize events; they would foster grandstanding on the part of the justices and lawyers; they would diminish the high esteem in which the Court is held; and the ensuing spectacle would make the judiciary appear political. The additional argument—which is, I suspect, the real one—is that it would invade the justices' privacy. If their faces became famous, they could no longer amble through antique shops unnoticed on summer mornings when the Court is in recess.

Fear of Soundbites

The distortion claim is an interesting one. Opponents of cameras in the Court worry that TV coverage would lead to tiny sound bites being rebroadcast; sound bites that would lose the complexity and nuance of an argument. In 1986, then-chief justice Warren Burger told a group of newspaper editors that he might conceivably allow cameras into the courtroom, but only if the proceedings were broadcast gavel-to-gavel. Among Burger's objections were that, without the enforced continuity, things would be taken out of context and distorted. Of course, the argument that you can't comprehend the highly technical and nuanced arguments before the Court is impossibly elitist. But if it's true that sound bites necessarily distort a process, why aren't the justices crusading against televised confirmation hearings? Do they think that the job interview can be "distorted" without consequence?. . .

The second argument—that cameras foster misbehavior— almost goes without saying. Think only of the O.J. Simpson trial. But if they foster bad behavior among senators, they may also promote good behavior among justices. If the justices knew, for instance, that they were being watched by millions of eyeballs, they might be less inclined to giggle among themselves at oral argument. Senators are generally running for reelection. So put them in front of a television camera and they have no choice but to go wild with their big hair and their big speeches. But Supreme Court justices are beholden to no one. They hold their seats for life. We have no mechanism to remove them. So why shouldn't we be entitled [to] monitor their job performance? Should they choose not to perform—to stare fixedly at the ceiling throughout oral argument as Clarence Thomas has been known to do—they suffer no consequences. And having a camera trained on them might just induce them to work harder.

Finally, consider the argument that televised hearings would diminish the esteem enjoyed by the judiciary, making the Court appear as political as the other branches. This is, when you stop to think about it, a rather bizarre claim: If nobody can see that we are political, they won't think we are political. Or as former chief justice William Rehnquist said in 1992, cameras "would lessen to a certain extent some of the mystique and moral authority" of the Supreme Court.

Now Greta Garbo is certainly entitled to worry about her mystique. But government officials should not be. Supreme Court justices may well worry that televisions in their church—I mean palace—I mean courtroom—would decrease the public esteem for the institution. I disagree: I believe that knowing what the justices do and how superbly they do it would only increase public approval of the Court. But more significantly, poll after poll shows the Court is held in extremely high esteem, whereas Congress is rated far lower. Taking the cameras out of the Senate and putting them in the courtroom would level the playing field, allowing the American public the opportunity to hate all three branches of government equally.

With respect to the argument—of course the Court is political. And it does the Court no good at all to be at its most secretive precisely when it is acting most ideologically. Consider that in November 2000, when Rehnquist rejected requests by several TV networks to televise the hearings in *Bush v. Gore*, he wrote in a letter to C-SPAN that "a majority of the Court" agreed that it was best to block the intrusion. But the consequence of keeping cameras out was to reinforce the idea that the fix was in, that the election was decided by a secret cabal of faceless jurists in a process so corrupt it needed to be kept secret. Precisely because the Court has inserted itself into the most hotly disputed questions, it should open up its activities to the public. It would serve to reassure Americans that there are immutable legal principles and processes undergirding their decisions, as opposed to judicial coin flips. The same is true for confirmation hearings: They appear political because they are political. Taking the cameras out may render them less political and more genuinely focused on truth-seeking. Unlike the justices, the senators vote their instinct, nothing more. And watching someone vote their instinct is like watching them eat snails. Why bother?

Finally, some of the justices worry that cameras in the courtroom would reduce decision making to cheap entertainment. Justice Antonin Scalia recently said, "I think there's something sick about making entertainment out of real people's legal problems." Scalia overestimates how interesting real people's problems are at the Supreme Court level, where there are no visible parties, no emotions, and no drama. This is not Judge Judy. Televising oral argument would violate no

The Public's Right to Know

[A bill to permit the Televising of Supreme Court Proceedings, S. 344] has been introduced in the Senate by Judiciary Committee Chairman Arlen Specter, R-Pa., that would allow sessions of the U.S. Supreme Court to be televised rather than just audio-taped as is now the practice. . . .

The purpose of Specter's legislation is to open the Supreme Court doors so that more Americans can see the process by which the Court reaches critical decisions of law that affect this country and everyday Americans. Because the Supreme Court of the United States holds power to decide cutting-edge questions on public policy, thereby effectively becoming a virtual "super legislature," the public has a right to know what the Supreme Court—and Antonin Scalia—is doing.

And that right would be substantially enhanced by televising the oral arguments of the Court so that the public can see and hear the issues presented to the Court. With this information, the public would have insight into key issues and be better equipped to understand the impact of the Court's decisions.

June Maxam, "Scalia Ban on Cameras in the Court Thwarts Judicial Acccountability," North Country Gazette, October 15, 2005.

one's privacy—with the exception of the nine sitting justices who are arguably already granted far more than they deserve.

Reluctant Celebrities

Which brings us to the real objection to cameras in the Court: The justices want their privacy. In 1996, Justice David Souter testified before Congress that "the day you see a camera come into our courtroom, it's going to roll over my dead body." Well, if we are going to grant the justices that privilege, we should certainly grant it to their future colleagues as well. Because, let's face it, confirmation hearings can be awkward: Nominees are grilled about their past jobs, their writings, and any possible ethical or moral lapse in their lifetimes. By contrast, oral argument is dry and doctrinal, far less invasive of the justices' privacy. Because it's not about them. (Well, maybe sometimes it's about Antonin Scalia.) If we want to protect judicial privacy, we should also protect the privacy of the lone nominee sitting in front of a circle of senators, being raked over the coals for grocery lists written 30 years ago. . . .

All of this ultimately raises the question: Why do the justices get to decide? Of course they don't want cameras to televise their jobs any more than I want a camera to televise mine. But what I do isn't a cornerstone of democracy. There was a time in which Congress made the same arguments for keeping C-SPAN at bay, but most of us now acknowledge that it is better for Congress (and for democracy) to promote openness and transparency; to trust citizens to watch and decide for themselves. And my guess is that after David Souter gets used to gaggles of middle-school girls clamoring for his autograph at Safeway, he'll learn to love the exposure, too. Celebrity is the price one pays for scoring a starring role in the life of this nation.

The stakes at a confirmation hearing are unbelievably high. These senators are placing an unelected official on the bench for a lifetime. But many justices—again, Clarence Thomas is an example—believe that oral argument doesn't have much impact on the justices' decisions in a case: they decide based on the briefs and precedent and closed-door sessions. Oral argument has one purpose: It is a tiny piece of theater to let the public in on the Court's work. So why not let the public in en masse? There is no point in public theater with such limited seating.

We need to start to be honest about the ways in which televised confirmation hearings are destroying the process. A

183

system that ought to be about truth-seeking and hard scrutiny has morphed into VH-1—with a focus on appearances to the exclusion of substance. This is no way to make decisions of so much moment to the country. At the same time, the events at oral argument are highly scripted and formal. There is no possibility of grandstanding on the part of the justices—they'll keep their jobs whether they are scintillating or soporific.

Pennsylvania Senator Arlen Specter has introduced a bill that would allow television cameras into the High Court. I would vote for that with one amendment: They should roll them right out of the judiciary committee room and across the street instead. Lights, camera, action!

> *"TV coverage of oral arguments would actually do a disservice to the public. Oral argument is arguably the least important part of any appeal. Far from offering a look into the issues of a case, oral argument more often than not resembles a janitorial sweeping of the dance floor after the party's over."*

Cameras Should Not Be Allowed in the U.S. Supreme Court

James N. Markels

James N. Markels is an attorney and a regular columnist for Brainwash, *a weekly online magazine of the America's Future Foundation, a nonprofit organization offering conservative and libertarian professionals opportunities to "publish, debate, strategize, reflect, govern, learn, and network." In this viewpoint, Markels argues that TV coverage of the oral arguments of the U.S. Supreme Court could be misleading to viewers who would not have access either to the substance of the legal briefs or to the conference room where the justices discuss the case.*

James N. Markels, "Lights, Camera, Supreme Court," *Brainwash*, April 30, 2006. Reproduced by permission.

As you read, consider the following questions:

1. Markels contends that TV coverage of U.S. Supreme Court oral arguments is a bad idea. In the author's opinion, what is the point of an oral argument before the Court?

2. Televising oral arguments before the U.S. Supreme Court would still leave viewers in the dark, according to Markels. Why does he contend that this is the case?

3. Audio recordings of oral arguments before the Supreme Court are already available to the public. In Markels's view, would video broadcasts accomplish more? Why or why not?

In a show of bravado in *The Washington Post*, Sen. Arlen Specter (R-Pa.) admonished the Supreme Court for daring to invalidate laws passed by Congress, and in retribution proposed the unthinkable—truly the "nuclear option" against the Court: video coverage of oral arguments.

Say it ain't so, Arlen.

If one wanted to come up with ways to get back at the Court, there are far better avenues than letting CNN set up shop in the courtroom. Like, say, making judicial appointments ten years rather than for life, or making the Justices "ride circuit" by serving on the Courts of Appeal during their vacation time in the summer. "The Real World: Supreme Court" just isn't that scary a proposition.

Cameras Won't Eliminate Corruption

Not to mention it's just a bad idea. Although Sen. Specter snaked Justice Brandeis' oft-cited quote, "Sunlight is . . . the best disinfectant," to argue that TV cameras would somehow compel the Justices to mend their evil ways, one only needs to look at C-SPAN's coverage of Congress to realize it did a piss-poor job of preventing the whole Abramoff mess. TV doesn't eliminate corruption; it only changes it.

Besides, TV coverage of oral arguments would actually do a disservice to the public. Oral argument is arguably the least important part of any appeal. Far from offering a look into the issues of a case, oral argument more often than not resembles a janitorial sweeping of the dance floor after the party's over.

Before the Justices even decide on whether to take a case or not, they've already had a law clerk analyze the facts and issues involved to determine whether the case poses a significant question worth resolving. A prime example of this is the "circuit split," where the Courts of Appeal have disagreed on a given legal issue. Then, if the Justices take the case, both sides of the case submit legal briefs on the issue that are usually quite exhaustive. (Remember, the case doesn't usually get to the Supreme Court until having slogged its way through a trial court and a Court of Appeal. Therefore, much argument over the legal issues has already been had.) By the time the Justices have read the entire record, the briefs, and the analysis of their clerks, you can rest assured that the Justices have a solid, if not complete, grasp on the case before them.

When coupled with the fact that the Justices all have extensive knowledge of the legal environment and have pretty well-thought-out views on the law already, the simple fact is that before appellant's counsel breathes one word in the hallowed courtroom, the Justices already know how they'll vote on the case. They might want to use argument to clear up a couple of things, but their view of the case is already established. It's all over but for the shouting.

So what is the point of oral argument? It's tradition, for the most part, and we lawyers love the art of vocal jujitsu. Even if the cause is lost, every lawyer wants to feel like they've had a chance to work some magic at the podium to save the day for their client, even if it's just a mirage.

More Law, Less Limelight

I know, I know, I'm a journalist. It is my solemn duty to scream "First Amendment" at every passerby, which can get quite tiring during the holiday shopping season. But to be fair, I'm not convinced that we truly need cameras in the Supreme Court.

Is the increased media exposure really necessary? In a society so entranced by celebrity, must we throw members of the Supreme Court into the mix? Am I the only one who remembers the [comedy sketch on *The Tonight Show*] Dancing Itos?

Cochran makes the exact argument you'd expect from a group of radio and television news directors. The public has the right to know—and see and hear, of course. But when balancing the scales between visual information versus extra publicity, I'm not convinced. . . .

It's pretty obvious that the Supreme Court is not and has never been in a rush to kick on the fresnels and power up the cameras. Seems like these public servants are more interested in the law than the limelight. Maybe we should keep it that way.

Mark J. Pescatore, *"Are Supreme Court Cameras Necessary?"*
Government Video, *December 1, 2005.*

TV Coverage Misleading

But that point would be lost on the public watching on TV. Not knowing the substance of the briefs and record already submitted to the Court, viewers might be led to believe that the decision of the case could hang on every word. If counsel stumbles a bit in the answer to a Justice's question, aha!, her side must be in trouble! Or if a Justice is slinging question after question at an advocate, perhaps that Justice is "on the fence." And if a Justice just sits there quietly (like Justice Thomas almost always does), what might that mean? That they haven't read the case?

While TV cameras can help the average channel-surfer get a feel for whether a given witness at trial is credible, there's just no corresponding insight into how the Court is going to go or should go. Some have proposed that whichever side gets more questions tends to be the side that loses, but even that's too rough and rude a ruler for something as sophisticated as the Court. Even veteran Court-watchers stand in awe of the opacity of the Court's poker face. Unless TV cameras were allowed in the conference room where the Justices discuss the cases after argument has been heard, we will still be in the dark. . . .

But you can bet that things would change on counsel's side. An advocate feeling that their side is weak might as well start grandstanding before the cameras as if the Justices were just another jury. Pithy quips that would get a stern eye from the bench might play well to the home crowd. How this helps the law is anybody's guess.

To be sure, this isn't about preserving the "majesty" of the Court. No TV camera could ever take that from it. But assuming the public understands the issue before the Court and is interested in hearing more about it (big assumptions, both), video broadcasts of oral argument would accomplish no more than the audio recordings already made available, and are actually more likely to lead the unsavvy viewer astray. And worst of all, from Sen. Specter's view, the Court still won't change a bit.

> *"Most experts agree that although juries generally do very well, they are influenced by pretrial publicity in ways that either lead them to be too hard on, or too soft on, famous defendants."*

Limits on Media Access to Celebrity Trials Is Appropriate

Dahlia Lithwick

Dahlia Lithwick is an author and a senior editor and legal correspondent for Slate. *She writes the column "Supreme Court Dispatches." She is the 2001 recipient of the Online News Association's award for online commentary. In this viewpoint, Lithwick contends that existing measures for keeping pretrial publicity at bay in celebrity trials are ineffective. She argues that drastic changes are necessary in the legal system to ensure that media coverage does not "tip the scales" of justice in celebrity trials.*

As you read, consider the following questions:

1. Lithwick cites several celebrity trials where she argues that the strategies meant to ensure an untainted jury pool were ineffective. What are some of the strategies she mentions?

2. In the 1807 trial of Aaron Burr for treason, what did Chief Justice John Marshall rule regarding the influence of the widespread publicity surrounding that trial?

3. Lithwick mentions the possibility of a "high-profile" specialty court as a way to remedy the problem of media influence on the outcome of a celebrity trial. What are some other legal circumstances where specialty courts are used?

The Scott Peterson trial changed venue, the Michael Jackson parties and their attorneys are (blessedly) gagged, Kobe Bryant's accuser's medical records are sealed, for now, and the Martha Stewart jurors have been carefully screened to keep out anyone who has ever socialized with her daughter, or slept on her 300-thread-count Embroidered Tambour sheets. Each of these strategies is meant to ensure an untainted jury pool in one of the dozen trials-of-the-century playing out on a cable network near you. Each is nearly comic in the scope of its ineffectiveness.

Does changing venue—moving a trial three Starbuckses north or two Old Navys south—really make a difference in an era of national, 24-hour, gavel-to-gavel news coverage? Maybe if the Peterson trial were relocated to the interior of the largest dormant volcano on Papua New Guinea, one could find a jury pool untainted by the relentless tabloid coverage and morass of misinformation available on the Internet. Does gagging Michael Jackson really change the fact that he is an icon, a legend—a wing nut, to be sure—but nevertheless able to summon the screaming fans and cameras necessary to transform an ordinary criminal proceeding into a music video ("The King of Pop's Limo-Top Dance Party & Arraignment")? Does the fact that Kobe Bryant's accuser hasn't been named in the mainstream media change the reality that you can click on a Web site and find her home address? And it was only after the presiding judge in the Martha Stewart trial had worked her way through all five boroughs in an attempt to find 12 jurors who'd never heard of a wire whisk that she was finally able to scrounge up a jury composed of the dozen local souls too preoccupied with Michael and Kobe to care about Martha.

"Strong Prejudices" or "Light Impressions"

These efforts to keep pretrial publicity at bay—at least long enough to select a jury—were inadequate back in 1807, when Aaron Burr went on trial for treason. His attorneys argued that it was impossible to find jurors who hadn't been influenced by the widespread publicity. Chief Justice John Marshall ultimately ruled that while jurors with "strong prejudices" could be excluded, "light impressions" based on prior knowledge of the case would be acceptable. Whether it's still possible to have light impressions in a tabloid world is not at all clear. Mark Twain, writing in 1875, was struck by the silliness of excluding any informed juror from a high-profile trial. "Why," he wrote, "could not the jury law be so altered as to give men of brains and honesty an equal chance with fools and miscreants?" And that was in an era where you could find untainted jurors so long as you affirmatively looked for people who didn't read. Those days are over. Jurors can be tainted just standing in the supermarket checkout aisles. (And jurors tainted by *Inside Edition* are vastly scarier than the "miscreants" decried by Twain.)

"Stone and Flint" Remedies

It's past time for us to agree that the tools afforded judges to control the effects of pretrial publicity (voir dire, sequestration, postponement, and absurd instructions to ignore that which you know to be true) are the legal equivalents of a stone and flint. If we are going to ensure that the rich and famous receive unbiased juries, we need to make some drastic changes to the legal system.

The threshold question is this: Do famous people really get off more easily than more obscure individuals? Alterna-

"The Court of Public Opinion"

A celebrity defendant has no choice. In contrast to mere mortals who become entangled in the criminal justice system, celebrity defendants face greater threats and enjoy substantial advantages. They can choose whether to leverage their fame and mobilize their fans to mitigate those threats and maximize those advantages—or not. But they can't ignore the unique calculus that applies only to celebrity trials. As the lawyers to the stars know full well, these considerations must be an essential element of their legal defense strategy. . . .

After all, despite the fact of their celebrity, these people are still criminal defendants whose fates will be decided on the evidence by an impartial jury. This concept, though quaint, rests somewhere between ideal and delusion. . . .

Today's media coverage is multiplied by more media outlets. But sheer volume does not alter the fundamental principle that defendants have a right to a public defense before trial and outside the courtroom. The difference between celebrity defendants, and the rest of us mere mortals, is that they can appear in the national media, if and when they so choose. The key question they, and their lawyers, must carefully consider is whether a nationally televised interview will do them, and their legal case, more harm than good.

"Litigating in the Limelight: Celebrity Defendants
Have Little Choice But to Try Their Cases in the
Court of Public Opinion," The Legal Times, *2004.*
www.decisionquest.com/litigation_library.php?NewsID=109.

tively, are jurors actually harder on them? Does it matter that celebrities may be able to buy themselves first-class justice, with fancy lawyers, expensive jury consultants, and top-notch PR experts? Or are juries too smart to fall for such manipulation? And even if the dynamic isn't real, should we worry that the public is certain that celebrities get off too easily?

The research is not at all conclusive, but most experts agree that although juries generally do very well, they are influenced by pretrial publicity in ways that either lead them to be too hard on, or too soft on, famous defendants. Empirical studies have shown that when juries perceive their verdict will be important, they will hold the prosecution to a higher standard of proof. One study from 1993 showed that jurors will be far more likely to acquit the attractive versus unattractive defendant. A 1976 study revealed that jurors find high-status defendants less blameworthy. A study in Basic and Applied Social Psychology revealed, interestingly, that black jurors are harder on black defendants, and white jurors go easier on white ones. One Northeastern University study showed that while athletes were arrested at a much higher rate than unknown defendants, the athletes were convicted at a significantly lower rate. Northeastern's and other studies also suggest that many assume that the famous and talented are either too good to behave badly, or that their victims are opportunists—witness the central defenses in both the Jackson and Bryant cases.

Celebrity in the Dock

Ultimately, it's hard to imagine not being influenced by the presence of a celebrity in the dock. Today, a controversial verdict can win a juror a round-trip to *Good Morning America*, instant fame (for doing something less vile than eating maggots), drinks with the defendant, and a lucrative book deal. So there are pretty powerful incentives to acquit. An O.J. Simpson juror reportedly got $57,000 from a book deal and TV interviews. And does anyone really want to be known as the guy who stole Kobe from the Lakers?

Since nothing can really be done about the media feeding-frenzy in this country we believe, and the courts have enshrined, the unfettered right to report on trials—we cannot muzzle the press. But if we can agree that this relentless media circus tips the scales, we should consider some changes to celebrity trials. The question thus becomes whether it's possible to normalize a celebrity trial.

One modest proposal: Let's give legal effect to the phrase "jury of one's peers."

What if we could impanel only jurors unimpressed with the magic of Neverland, or indifferent to the prospect of hobnobbing with NBA athletes? It could happen. In a curious accident, among the 85 potential jurors in Robert Blake's murder trial, two of the folks filling out questionnaires last January were Christina Applegate and Harry Shearer—actors who would justifiably be less impressed with Baretta's star power than their own. But lesser lights, if sufficiently jaded, would also qualify. We live in a time when the semitalented, the formerly talented, and the never-to-be-talented all can find steady TV work, so it's likely that a panel of washed-up, world-weary former stars would be delighted to perform their civic duty by sitting in judgment over one of their own.

Specialty Courts

Specialty courts are increasingly in vogue: bankruptcy courts, family courts, drug courts, science courts. An article in the *Indiana Law Journal* sensibly calls for the establishment of "high-profile Courts," with handpicked judges specially trained to deal with the media. They would have lifetime appointments (and would thus not be susceptible to public pressure) and extensive experience with celebrity trials—so that the famous could waive their right to a jury trial and be tried by a bored, disaffected judge. An improvement on this system would be to create a celebrity court in which that disaffected judge joined forces with semifamous jurors. It's not inconceivable that Michael Jackson might get a fair trial at the hands of, say, Pee

Wee Herman, Boy George, Robert Downey Jr., Winona Ryder, Rush Limbaugh, and Kato Kaelin. The weird judged by peers of weirdness.

At common law, jurors were selected precisely because they knew the facts of the case and the parties. Since the minds and choices of modern celebrities are more incomprehensible than particle physics, it makes sense to return to that practice in high-profile cases. But we need real insiders; modern jurors think they know the parties, when all they really know is the spin.

Ultimately, there aren't many ways for us to brace against the prejudicial frenzy that comes with a celebrity trial. Except perhaps to remind ourselves that one can be gorgeous, or talented, or a Jackson, and still not be entitled to simply take what one wants. While it's not known whether any of the stars on trial this year committed the crimes alleged, it would go a long way toward serving real justice to be assured of a jury more interested in truth than an autograph.

> *"More and more . . . courts and parties in high-profile cases are turning the First Amendment upside down by urging and imposing greater secrecy the greater the public interest in the case. Public access often is treated as an inconvenience, an intrusion, or a barrier to achieving a fair trial."*

Limits on Media Access to Celebrity Trials Is Unfair

Theodore J. Boutrous Jr. and Michael H. Dore

Theodore J. Boutrous Jr. and Michael H. Dore are attorneys with the media practice group Gibson, Dunn & Crutcher. They represented a coalition of major news organizations in the celebrity trial of singer Michael Jackson. In this viewpoint, the authors contend that in high-profile celebrity cases, the constitutional right of access should not be diminished, nor is celebrity status sufficient to defeat the First Amendment presumption that "openness will enhance fairness."

As you read, consider the following questions:

1. The authors contend that public scrutiny of the justice system is not self-defeating and that heightened public interest in high-profile cases should be valued. Why do they see this as important?

2. According to the authors, the First Amendment imposes a heavy burden on those who advocate for courtroom secrecy. What conditions must be shown before any part of a judicial record may be sealed or a hearing closed?

3. The authors contend that courts used a double standard during the high-profile trials of Kobe Bryant, Martha Stewart, and Michael Jackson. According to the authors, what did the courts hold to justify secrecy in these cases?

The symbolic figure of Blind Justice presides over courthouses throughout the country. Inside the courtroom, however, there is a growing trend to apply two different standards of justice: one for celebrities and one for everybody else. In recent high-profile cases, secrecy has supplanted the public's constitutional right of access, with courts doing everything they can to close the proceedings and information related to the case. The prosecutions of Kobe Bryant, Martha Stewart, and Michael Jackson are perhaps the most prominent examples of this troubling approach.

But public scrutiny of the justice system is not self-defeating. The constitutional right of access should not be diminished by a defendant's star power, and, if anything, heightened public interest should be valued for the light it shines on the particular proceeding and the judicial process in general. . . .

More and more, however, courts and parties in high-profile cases are turning the First Amendment upside down by urging and imposing greater secrecy the greater the public interest in the case. Public access often is treated as an inconvenience, an intrusion, or a barrier to achieving a fair trial, while local officials seek to charge the media huge parking and other fees simply for doing their jobs of covering judicial proceedings and reporting the news to the public. There is a very real trend toward litigants and courts acting as though the dissemination of basic, official information about a legal proceeding is an inherent evil that must be prevented. As a result, the parties routinely request, and the courts too often grant, orders imposing wide-ranging secrecy in a number of contexts. Voir dire and other court proceedings are closed to the public. Traditionally public court records, like indictments and exhibits entered into evidence, are sealed. Even prior restraints, almost universally rejected in the law, are imposed and upheld. In effect, the presumption of openness mandated by the Constitution is being reversed, and intense public interest in a high-profile trial is identified, explicitly or implicitly, as the reason why.

No Celebrity Secrets

Celebrity trials are entitled to no such additional secrecy. Courts in these cases are rightly concerned about protecting the defendant's fair trial rights and often face challenges in doing so, but that does not justify cutting off the free flow of information to the public. The First Amendment presumes that openness will enhance fairness, and it imposes a heavy burden on those who seek to defeat that presumption. Among other things, advocates for secrecy must make a very specific, compelling, narrowly targeted showing that an overriding interest will be injured before any part of a judicial record may be sealed or a hearing closed. There simply is no celebrity exception to these exacting constitutional standards that govern in every other case.

As the U.S. Supreme Court has noted, "the sure knowledge that *anyone* is free to attend gives assurance that established

Celebrity Privacy Versus Public Justice

High-profile Americans—whether from the ranks of entertainment, politics or business—routinely lay claim to special treatment before the courts because of their fame, position or power. Incredibly, some judges grant that special status. The trial judge in the Martha Stewart case shut the public out of the jury-selection process in a decision overturned by a higher court. The trial judge in the Kobe Bryant case imposed an unprecedented prior restraint on the press, a decision upheld by the Colorado Supreme Court. And a unanimous U.S. Supreme Court sanctioned the notion that the survivors of the famous or infamous share their privacy rights. . . .

All of us value our privacy and in many ways identify with those caught up in the privacy-rending mill of a newsworthy court case. But no one knows when or where this idea of one person's privacy trumping the First Amendment rights of the public and the press will end. We can hope that it will stop somewhere short of private justice, conducted in secret, for the rich and famous.

Paul K. McMasters,
"Celebrity Privacy Claims Trump Public Justice,"
American Press Institute, *July 30, 2004.*
www.Americanpressinstitute.org.

procedures are being followed and that deviations will become known." Openness, therefore, "enhances both the basic fairness of the criminal trial and the appearance of fairness so essential to public confidence in the system."

The courts have established specific procedures and standards to protect this important First Amendment interest. . . .

First Amendment Head Stand

In the recent high-profile cases involving Kobe Bryant, Martha Stewart, and Michael Jackson, however, courts have, in essence, held that the greater the public interest in judicial records and proceedings, the greater the need for secrecy—a dangerous and unsupported proposition that turns the First Amendment on its head. These courts have eschewed more narrowly tailored alternatives to secrecy, such as rigorous voir dire, to ensure an unbiased jury. Instead, they have invoked the heightened public interest to justify extraordinarily broad orders closing proceedings, sealing judicial records, and imposing prior restraints on trial participants and, in one instance, even on the press. Such a double standard, which allows celebrities to litigate in secret and keep details off the public record, is deeply troubling and plainly violates the First Amendment. . . .

Secrecy Fosters Public Suspicion

Courts in recent high-profile cases have used the interest generated by those proceedings to prevent the public from serving its traditional role as a vigilant guardian of fairness in the criminal justice system. Even if such secrecy is designed to serve the understandable goals of protecting an alleged victim of sexual assault or a defendant's right to a fair trial, constitutional requirements must be respected. Celebrity status does not demand an exception to the First Amendment standards that govern in every other case, and the public's right of access is not diminished by heightened interest in the proceedings. To hold otherwise, as is the trend in celebrity cases, fosters public suspicion and misunderstanding, casting a shadow over a system that derives its strength from openness and transparency.

> *"Nowadays, we do not turn on the television or read the newspapers to watch the latest political and social developments, but rather to catch up on the day's scandal and gossip. We do not turn to the media to inform us about court cases in a thorough and thoughtful way, but rather to be thrilled and entertained. Today, the media presents to us, the public, the notorious cases of our day and we are called upon to make up our minds, to decide these cases, to reach our own verdicts."*

Media Coverage of Trials Should Inform, Not Merely Entertain

Steven I. Platt

Steven I. Platt is an associate judge on the Prince George's County Circuit Court. He writes a regular column for The Daily Record *called "The Pursuit of Justice." In this viewpoint, Platt argues that many of the issues that come before U.S. courts go to*

Steven I. Platt, "Commentary: Managing the Relationship Between an Independent Judiciary and Free Media," *The Daily Record*, July 8, 2006. Reproduced by permission of the author.

the very heart of our political, economic, social, and cultural order. The media, he argues, can and should strive to explain the constitutional and statutory rights of the accused, rather than focus on the "sexier, racier aspects" in high-profile cases.

As you read, consider the following questions:

1. Platt argues judges are expected to exercise wise judgment in complex disputes of increasing complexity where demagogues and talk shows provide simplistic and shallow answers. According to Platt, are judges always allowed to explain or defend themselves from criticism after rendering unpopular decisions?
2. In Platt's view, what is the indispensable role of the judiciary?
3. What process serves as a check on the judicial branch of government? Which agency handles ethical problems that may arise with a judge?

In recent years, courts throughout the nation have been faced with an ever-rising tide of litigation. Many of the issues raised go to the very heart of our political, economic, social, and cultural order.

They bring to the courts disputes that often involve more than mere legal disputes. There are questions involving civil rights, the breakdown of social and family values, threats to the environment and to the health and well-being of the public, the cost of energy and many more.

We are witnessing great conflict and accompanying stress in our society between groups that take moral and religious positions on matters involving abortion, the right to die, the death penalty, pornography, sexual conduct and crime. I need not list all of the topics to make the point that many of these and other issues are being fought out in the courts—or around decisions made by courts.

In the areas of domestic violence and crime, judges—pressed by growing numbers of disputes of increasing complexity—are expected to do what no one else can do. They are expected to predict the unpredictable: the vagaries of human behavior. They are expected to exercise wise judgment in the areas where demagogues and talk shows provide simplistic and shallow answers. After rendering those decisions, judges are ethically constrained from explaining or even defending themselves against vituperative criticism if those decisions prove, with hindsight, to be unpopular with the media or with other branches of government.

Is this all new? Certainly not.

Over 300 years ago, we endured witchcraft trials because the public demanded them. Ultimately, they ceased because that same public, repulsed by the results of what they had earlier demanded, withdrew its support for these trials and the courts who heard them.

Witchcraft Trials?

In the last few years, I have sometimes felt like we are once again living in a time of witchcraft trials. This time, however, they are brought to us electronically.

Nowadays, we do not turn on the television or read the newspapers to watch the latest political and social developments, but rather catch up on the day's scandal and gossip. We do not turn to the media to inform us about court cases in a thorough and thoughtful way, but rather to be thrilled and entertained. Today, the media presents to us, the public, the notorious cases of our day and we are called upon to make up our minds, to decide these cases, to reach our own verdicts.

Who did not make up his or her mind, one way or the other, about O. J. Simpson after the exhaustive media coverage given to that case?

Focusing on the more mundane cases that the courts of Maryland consider daily, who is not outraged at the supposed failure of the court system and its judges when a domestic violence restraining order is issued but does not prove to be effective at keeping a stalker away from their victim?

I will not comment on the merits of a particular case. But it is proper for me to observe that these examples demonstrate that reporters, opinion writers, talk-show hosts, television stations and, yes, newspapers lead citizens to believe that the media provide all the relevant facts of a particular case and it is for them to make a decision.

The problem, however, is that it is not within the province of the media or of the public to decide these cases. I remind our readers of Henry David Thoreau's words in his work on civil disobedience. He said, "A government in which the majority rules in all cases cannot be based on justice, even as far as men understand it."

This wisdom was in the minds of the drafters of our state and federal constitutions. Despite the tendency of many today to forget it, our government is not a democracy in the sense that the popular will is to prevail in every matter. Our government is a constitutional representative democracy where the minority is offered protection from the tyranny of the majority, and individuals are protected from government by the Bill of Rights.

It is a government not only of checks and balances, but one of limitation and constraint between the individual citizen and the government—even if government reflects the will of the majority of the day. The indispensable role of the judiciary is to preserve that balance.

I know that scandal sells and that the media is doing nothing it's prohibited from doing, but I suggest the media is not necessarily doing the right thing

If liberty is the sum of all rights of a member of an organized civil society concurrent with the guaranteed protection

A Remarkable Absence of Context and Perspective

An unexpected range of otherwise respectable news organizations devoted a stunning number of column inches and broadcast minutes to covering the hearing at which Superior Court Judge Michael T. Sauer sentenced [Paris] Hilton to 45 days in jail for violating the probation she received for driving while under the influence of alcohol. Their coverage—and nearly all the extensive commentary that accompanied it—was remarkable not only for its volume, but also for the absence of most of the context and perspective serious newspaper and broadcast journalists usually deem essential when reporting on the criminal justice system.

Nobody in the mainstream media, for example, bothered to inquire very deeply into whether Sauer's sentence was within the usual range for such an offense. . . .

Sauer had decided to make an example of a spoiled young woman who was behaving as if her celebrity put her above the law—and it was an impression both the serious and tabloid press seemed to relish.

The tabloid press is somebody else's problem but it's troubling that none of the mainstream print or broadcast journalists commenting on the case pointed out that the American criminal justice system does not make examples of people. It penalizes people for specific individual acts and punishes them according to the law. We do not punish one person to instruct others. We rely on the public administration of disinterested and dispassionate justice to educate and deter.

"Paris Isn't the Only One Guilty,"
Los Angeles Times, *May 12, 2007.*
www.latimes.com.

against interference [with] those rights, and license is liberty abused, then we now seem to be moving toward a system where license is preferred over liberty.

Now, in my view, the electronic media in general are much more into the scandal game than are the newspapers. Fortunately, I still see thoughtful and informative coverage of today's events from the print media, particularly professional and business publications. But I also see room for improvement, especially where coverage of the court system and the law is concerned.

Media Fails to Explain

The primary problem I see is that the media does not explain the nature of the judicial system; the emphasis is on the sexier, racier aspects of the story. Most of the time the competition between the lawyers, the reaction of the public and the litigants, and the personalities involved are described and analyzed, not the dispute itself or the important ideas underlying the dispute.

High-profile cases are not fictitious creations or even literary works intended to entertain. Rather, they are very real events significantly affecting the lives of those involved and calling into play our constitutional system of ordered government.

I believe that reporters and editors can and should strive to treat these cases as such. Furthermore, I do not think doing so will necessarily detract from the story being told, sell fewer newspapers or reduce commercial interest in the media enterprise or outlet.

In my opinion, coverage of an infamous crime should include an explanation of the constitutional and statutory rights of the accused. This coverage should not reduce those rights to mere legal technicalities that clever defense attorneys use to get their clients off. Those rights protect all of us and they are the only feature distinguishing our form of government from an abusive system of government. Indeed, it is the court system that the media often call upon to protect their own constitutional rights.

We should never forget that Hitler, Stalin, the apartheid government of South Africa and every dictator and regime of recent history has known this fact. It is no accident that every malevolent authoritarian has sought to seize control of the judiciary—especially the criminal courts—one of the first acts necessary to consolidate dictatorial power over the people. The message is clear. A strong, independent judiciary is the bulwark of liberty and social justice.

A Bulwark of Liberty

I cannot, however, be intellectually honest in this space, which is provided after all by a newspaper, and hold the media completely to blame for the problems I am discussing. I know the media periodically has problems with access to information in the court system and that many reporters and editors believe that the judiciary is not held to the standard of accountability that it should be required to adhere to.

Historically, the courts have not been exemplary in distributing information to the media and to the public. We have not done the best job of making the courts accessible and understandable. Furthermore, the general reluctance of many judges to talk to the media and the ethical constraints which prohibit us in some cases from doing so, without question, contribute to the problems I have focused on.

So, yes, more needs to be done by judges. But if judges are to open up, an effort by the media must be evident. The judicial branch of government is different from the executive and legislative branches. When judges make substantive mistakes in their judicial work, they are checked and corrected by the appellate process.

The Judicial Disability Commission handles ethical problems and, where appropriate, sanctions or even removes a judge from office. No such checks are available to correct illegal or incorrect decisions of officials of the other two branches of government. Nor is there any legal mechanism, short of impeachment, to remove an elected official of either the legislative or executive branches of government.

What we need is greater understanding and communication. A reporter should not have to contend with judges who believe that they are above scrutiny, and reporters should not have to be in good graces with clerical employees of the courts in order to get information that is supposed to be available to the public. The judicial system, on the other hand, should not be recklessly attacked and put in low public esteem or be subject to unwarranted scorn.

With that being my closing comment in this column, I cannot help being reminded of a quote I have always appreciated from Goethe, which, if I may paraphrase, illustrates perhaps the basic point of this column. That point is that the judiciary will always be at war with what it ought to be. Recognizing that, it is the media and the journalist's job to describe to the public what judges and the judiciary are. Nevertheless, when a reporter or an editor describes what a judge does, the reporter or editor could also explain what the judge and court ought to do and how the system should work. Then, perhaps, the judiciary will some day be what it ought to be.

Periodical Bibliography

The following articles have been selected to supplement the diverse views presented in this chapter.

Amanda Buck | "Shuttered Justice: Momentum Is Gaining on Allowing Cameras into Federal Courtrooms," *The News Media & The Law*, vol. 30, no. 1, Winter 2006, www.rcfp.org.

Center for Individual Freedom | "U.S. Supreme Court, Blind Justice?" January 9, 2004, www.cfif.org.

Dick Dahl | "Trial in the Press, Duke Lacrosse Case Latest Example of a Growing Trend," *Lawyers USA*, July 17, 2006.

Matthew Gilbert | "Order in the Court—In Our Reality-Mad Culture, It's Reassuring to Hear Judges Say No to Cameras," *Boston Globe*, April 4, 2004, www.boston.com.

Monica King | "A Camera in the U.S. Supreme Court? Absolutely!" *American Chronicle*, November 14, 2005, www.americanchronicle.com.

Jane Kirtley | "The Blog and the Ban: An American Blogger Strikes a Blow for Freedom of Information in Canada," *American Journalism Review*, June–July 2005, www.ajr.org.

Jessica Martin | "High-profile Celebrity Trials Test Lawyers' Skills with Unique Set of Challenges," *Washington University in St. Louis*, February 10, 2004, http://newsinfo.wustl.edu.

Corey Pein | "Celebrity Justice—At Big-Name Trials, the Press Is Paying in More Ways than One," *Columbia Journalism Review*, no. 6, November–December 2004, www.cjrarchives.org.

David Stras | "Can Congress Mandate Cameras in the Courtroom?" *SCOTUS Blog*, Supreme Court of the United States Blog, May 28, 2007, www.scotusblog.com.

For Further Discussion

Chapter 1

1. President George W. Bush has praised the USA Patriot Improvement and Reauthorization Act for providing necessary tools for the military, law enforcement, homeland security, and intelligence professionals to protect Americans from terrorist threats. The American Civil Liberties Union (ACLU) contends that some sections of the Patriot Act violate fundamental American freedoms. In your opinion, does the USA Patriot Act compromise civil rights in the interest of security? Is this ever a necessity?

2. According to a press release from the office of the White House press secretary, the Military Commissions Act of 2006 will allow the CIA to continue questioning key terrorist leaders and operatives and provide for the prosecution of foreign terrorists accused of war crimes through full and fair trials. Anthony Romero, by contrast, argues that this legislation is "one of the worst civil liberties measures ever enacted in American history." Which viewpoint provides the more convincing argument, and why?

3. Michelle E. Boardman argues that presidential signing statements have long been an essential part of the constitutional dialogue between governmental branches. Jennifer Van Bergen, by contrast, contends that President George W. Bush has used signing statements to expand executive power in violation of the fundamental principle of separation of powers. In your view, should limits be placed on the use of presidential signing statements? What criteria might ensure the proper balance for separation of powers?

4. Ezekiel Edwards contends that the DNA exoneration of over two hundred people, serving a total of 2,475 years in

prison for crimes they did not commit, proves that the justice system is flawed. William C. Thompson, however, argues that many errors occur in the performing of DNA tests, and there is no guarantee of accurate results. In your opinion, what measures are necessary to ensure that wrongful convictions do not occur? How do you think DNA results could be made more reliable in criminal cases?

Chapter 2

1. Peter Vaira argues that the powers of the federal grand jury are necessary tools for investigation and prosecution of criminal wrongdoing and political corruption. Richard Alexander and Sheldon Portman, however, contend that grand jury powers are abusive and that individuals called before a grand jury are denied certain rights necessary to their defense. In your opinion, are the powers of a grand jury excessive? What are the benefits of such a system?

2. Sherry F. Colb argues that a peremptory strike against a potential juror based on religious affiliation is an acceptable challenge in the jury selection process. Robert T. Miller, however, holds the view that peremptory strikes based on religion may be a violation of the Constitution's equal protection clause. In your opinion, which argument is most convincing? Why?

Chapter 3

1. Alberto J. Mora and Thomas R. Pickering defend the right of habeas corpus as the preeminent safeguard of individual liberty. They argue that the Military Commissions Act of 2006 limits that vital right. By contrast, Joseph Klein contends that habeas corpus was never intended as an "absolute right that must be made available even to our

avowed foreign enemies during war." In your view, should habeas corpus rights be extended to all prisoners regardless of status and location?

2. The American Friends Service Committee argues on behalf of immigrants that full recognition and protection of human rights should be granted to all people, documented or undocumented. Lou Dobbs argues that any plan for legalization "would open our borders to tens of millions of people with the potential to change the course of American history." What is your opinion about the probable results of granting legal status to undocumented residents?

3. Plea Bargain agreements are the method most often used to settle legal cases in U.S. courtrooms. Grant D. Griffiths argues that plea bargain agreements are necessary. Timothy Lynch contends that plea bargain agreements thwart due process constitutional protections afforded to defendants and must be abolished. Given the overwhelming number of cases that crowd U.S. court dockets, is the waiving of due process rights through plea bargain agreements the only solution?

Chapter 4

1. Internet Bloggers increasingly seek access to U.S. courtrooms. The Internet Blog, *A Progressive on the Prairie*, argues that journalist access to courtroom proceedings should be open to Internet bloggers and not be limited to otherwise credentialed reporters. James McGrath Morris, by contrast, contends that some standards and protections that characterize mainstream journalism may be compromised if Internet bloggers have equal access in the courtroom. Do you think that Internet bloggers should be held to traditional journalistic standards? Why or why not?-

2. June Maxim, a proponent of judicial accountability, contends that televising the oral arguments of the Supreme Court will allow the public insight into key issues that would facilitate an understanding of the impact of the Court's decisions. James N. Markels disagrees. He argues that televising oral arguments of Supreme Court justices would only serve to confuse viewers who would not have access to full discussion of the issues. In your view, would cameras in the Supreme Court provide a necessary public service and promote justice? Why or why not?

3. Media coverage of celebrity trials, in Dahlia Lithwick's view, may prejudice the outcome. She suggests special "celebrity courts," as a remedy. Theodore J. Boutrous Jr. and Michael H. Dore contend that limiting media access in celebrity trials is an unfair restriction. Steven I. Platt contends that media responsibility in court proceedings should focus on content and context, with emphasis on explaining the rights in question, rather than on the entertainment value of celebrity trials. How do you think the media can best serve the public in high-profile trials?

Organizations to Contact

The editors have compiled the following list of organizations concerned with the issues debated in this book. The descriptions are derived from materials provided by the organizations. All have publications or information available for interested readers. The list was compiled on the date of publication of the present volume; names, addresses, phone and fax numbers, and e-mail and Internet addresses may change. Be aware that many organizations take several weeks or longer to respond to inquiries, so allow as much time as possible.

American Center for Law and Justice (ACLJ)
P.O. Box 90555, Washington, DC   20090-0555
(757) 226-2489 • fax: (757) 226-2836
Web site: www.aclj.org

The ACLJ specializes in constitutional law and is specifically dedicated to the ideal that religious freedom and freedom of speech are inalienable rights. The center's purpose is to educate, promulgate, conciliate, and where necessary, litigate to ensure that those rights are protected under the law. The organization has participated in numerous cases before the Supreme Court, federal court of appeals, federal district courts, and various state courts regarding freedom of religion and freedom of speech.

American Conservative Union (ACU)
1007 Cameron Street, Alexandria, VA   22314
(703) 836-8602 • fax: (703) 836-8606
Web site: www.conservative.org

The American Conservative Union is the nation's oldest and largest grassroots conservative lobbying organization. ACU's purpose is to communicate and advance the goals and principles of conservatism through one multi-issue, umbrella organization. ACU is committed to a market economy, the doctrine of original intent of the framers of the Constitution, traditional moral values, and a strong national defense.

American Grand Jury Foundation (AGJF)

P.O. Box 1690, Modesto, CA   95353-1690
(877) 563-6163
Web site: www.grandjuryfoundation.org

The American Grand Jury Foundation is dedicated to encouraging responsible and effective interventions by grand jurors and other citizens into local government affairs. AGJF is a nonprofit corporation that pursues its objectives through a nonpolitical and nonpartisan research and publication program.

American Immigration Law Foundation

918 F Street NW, 6th Floor, Washington, DC   20004
(202) 742-5600 • fax: (202) 742-5619
e-mail: info@ailf.org
Web site: www.ailf.org

The American Immigration Law Foundation is dedicated to increasing public understanding of immigration law and policy and the value of immigration to the United States, and to advancing fundamental fairness and due process under the law for immigrants.

American Judicature Society

The Opperman Center at Drake University
2700 University Avenue, Des Moines, IA   50311
(515) 271-2281 • fax: (515) 279-3090
e-mail: sandersen@ajs.org
Web site: www.ajs.org

The American Judicature Society works through its Center for Judicial Independence to fulfill its mission to promote a judiciary that is free to, and that does in fact, render decisions based solely on the law and the facts of each case, without bowing to popular, political, or other extraneous pressures.

Bill of Rights Defense Committee

8 Bridge Street, Suite A, Northampton, MA   01060
(413) 582-0110
e-mail: info@bordc.org
Web site: www.bordc.org

The BORDC's mission is to promote, organize, and support a diverse, effective, nonpartisan national grassroots movement to restore and protect the civil rights and liberties guaranteed by the Bill of Rights.

Fair Trial Initiative

201 W. Main Street, Suite 300, Durham, NC   27701
(919) 680-2986 • fax: (919) 688-7973
Web site: www.fairtrial.org

The Fair Trial Initiative works to confront systemic inequalities in the criminal justice system and help resolve the crisis of incompetent trial counsel for indigent defendants facing the death penalty by funding fellowships for recent law school graduates to work with underfunded trial counsel in capital cases, providing pro bono opportunities for associates at law firms to work on capital trials, and facilitating other opportunities related to counsel for indigent defendants.

Foundation for Defense of Democracies

P.O. Box 33249, Washington, DC   20033
(202) 207-0190 • fax: (202) 207-0191
e-mail: info@defenddemocracy.org
Web site: www.defenddemocracy.org

The Foundation for Defense of Democracies is a nonpartisan policy institute dedicated exclusively to "promoting pluralism, defending democratic values, and fighting the ideologies that drive terrorism," through research, communications, education, and investigative journalism.

Fully Informed Jury Association (FIJA)
American Jury Institute, P.O. Box 5570
Helena, MT   59604-5570
(406) 442-7800 • fax: (406) 442-9332
e-mail: aji@fija.org
Web site: www.fija.org

The FIJA works to restore and protect the role of the juror and the institution of trial by jury. The organization sponsors educational seminars for legal professionals, publishes commentary, develops and presents amicus briefs when the institution of the jury is at issue, provides interviews to the media, speaks at functions and in classrooms, and distributes educational literature. FIJA publishes the quarterly magazine *The American Juror*.

Future of Freedom Foundation
11350 Random Hills Road, Suite 800, Fairfax, VA   22030
(703) 934-6101 • fax: (703) 352-8678
e-mail: fff@fff.org

The Future of Freedom Foundation is a Libertarian organization that works to advance freedom by providing an uncompromising moral and economic case for individual liberty, free markets, private property, and limited government. The foundation produces *Freedom Daily*, a journal of libertarian essays.

Hudson Institute
1015 Fifteenth Street NW, 6th Floor, Washington, DC   20005
(202) 974-2400 • fax: (202) 974-2410
e-mail: info@hudson.org
Web site: www.hudson.org

The Hudson Institute is a nonpartisan public policy research organization that forecasts trends and develops solutions for governments, businesses, and the public. Through publications, conferences, and policy recommendations, the institute seeks to guide global leaders in government and business.

Innocence Project
100 Fifth Avenue, 3rd Floor, New York, NY   10011
(212) 364-5340
e-mail: info@innocenceproject.org
Web site: www.innocenceproject.org

The Innocence Project is a nonprofit legal clinic and criminal justice resource center that works to exonerate the wrongfully convicted through post-conviction DNA testing and to develop and implement reforms to prevent wrongful convictions.

Institute for the Advancement of the American Legal System (IAALS)
University of Denver, 2044 E. Evans Avenue, #307
Denver, CO   80208
(303) 871-6600 • fax: (303) 871-6610
e-mail: legalinstitute@du.edu
Web site: www.du.edu/legalinstitute

The Institute for the Advancement of the American Legal System at the University of Denver is a nonpartisan, legal reform organization devoted to targeting dysfunctional areas of the system and offering innovative, real-world solutions. IAALS conducts research on topics ranging from judicial accountability to family law and develops specific, actionable recommendations. IAALS also hosts regular forums to highlight emerging issues and facilitate dialogue among legal scholars, practitioners, and the community at large.

Judicial Watch
P.O. Box 44444, Washington, DC   20026
(888) 593-8442 • fax (202) 646-5199
e-mail: info@judicialwatch.org
Web site: www.judicialwatch.org

Judicial Watch is a conservative, nonpartisan educational foundation working to promote transparency, accountability, and integrity in government, politics, and the law. Judicial Watch seeks to ensure that political and judicial officials do not abuse the powers entrusted to them by the American people and fulfills its educational mission through litigation, investigations, and public outreach.

National Center for Courts and Media
National Judicial College Building/MS 358, Reno, NV 89557
(775) 327-8270 • fax: (775) 327-2160
e-mail: info@judges.org
Web site: www.judges.org/nccm

The National Center for Courts and Media is an information source about the interaction between the working press and U.S. courts. The center was formed by the National Judicial College in collaboration with the Reynolds School of Journalism at the University of Nevada.

National Criminal Justice Association (NCJA)
720 Seventh Street NW, 3rd Floor, Washington, DC 20001
(202) 628-8550 • fax: (202) 628-0080
e-mail: info@ncja.org
Web site: www.ncja.org

The NCJA mission is "to promote the development of justice systems in states, tribal nations, and units of local government that enhance public safety; prevent and reduce the harmful effects of criminal and delinquent behavior on victims, individuals and communities; adjudicate defendants and sanction offenders fairly and justly." The NCJA serves as the formal mechanism for informing the Congress of state, tribal, and local criminal and juvenile justice needs and accomplishments.

National Equal Justice Library
Georgetown University Law Center, 111 G Street NW
Washington, DC 20001
(304) 535-6985 • fax: (202) 274-4365
e-mail: contact@equaljusticelibrary.org
Web site: http://equaljusticelibrary.org

The National Equal Justice Library is a joint project of the American Bar Association, the American Association of Law Libraries, the National Legal Aid and Defender Association, and Georgetown University's Law Center, dedicated to "honoring and advancing the pursuit of equal justice and the role of counsel for the poor," by rescuing, collecting, and preserving unique materials that document the history of the struggle to provide equal justice for all, by making the collections available to the public, by hosting educational programs, and by inspiring this and future generations of lawyers to serve the poor.

National Lawyers Guild

132 Nassau Street, Rm. 922, New York, NY   10038
(212) 679-5100 • fax: 212-679-2811
e-mail: director@nlg.org
Web site: www.nlg.org

The National Lawyers Guild is dedicated to the need for basic and progressive change in the structure of our political and economic system. Through its members—lawyers, law students, jailhouse lawyers, and legal workers united in chapters and committees—the guild works locally, nationally, and internationally as an effective political and social force in the service of the people.

Reporters Committee for Freedom of the Press (RCFP)

1101 Wilson Blvd., Suite 1100, Arlington, VA   22209
(800) 336-4243
e-mail: rcfp@rcfp.org
Web site: www.rcfp.org

The Reporters Committee for Freedom of the Press is a nonprofit organization dedicated to providing free legal assistance to journalists since 1970. The committee publishes the quarterly magazine, *The News Media & the Law*.

Bibliography of Books

Howard
Abadinsky

Law and Justice: An Introduction to the American Legal System. 6th ed. Paramus, NJ: Prentice Hall, 2006.

Jeffrey F. Addicott

Cases and Materials on Terrorism Law. 3rd ed. Tucson, AZ: Lawyers & Judges Publishing, 2006.

Robert M. Bloom

Ratting: The Use and Abuse of Informants in the American Justice System. Westport, CT: Praeger, 2002.

James Bovard

Terrorism and Tyranny: Trampling Freedom, Justice, and Peace to Rid the World of Evil. New York: St. Martin's Press, 2003.

Jon Bruschke and
William E. Loges

Free Press vs. Fair Trials: Examining Publicity's Role in Trial Outcomes. London: Lawrence Erlbaum Associates, 2005.

Stephen B.
Burbank and
Barry Friedman,
eds.

Why Judicial Independence Matters. Thousand Oaks, CA: Sage Publications, 2002.

Phillip Cooper

By Order of the President: The Use and Abuse of Executive Direct Action. Lawrence, KS: University Press of Kansas, 2002.

Jim Dwyer, Peter
Neufed, and
Barry Scheck

Actual Innocence. New York: Doubleday, 2000.

Eric M. Freedman · *Habeas Corpus: Rethinking the Great Writ of Liberty.* New York: New York University Press, 2003.

Glenn Greenwald · *How Would a Patriot Act? Defending American Values from a President Run Amok.* Working Assets Publishing, 2006.

David Lazer · *DNA and the Criminal Justice System: The Technology of Justice.* Boston: MIT Press, 2004.

Jon Lipsky, Wes McKinley, Jacque Brever, et al. · *The Ambushed Grand Jury Citizens' Investigation: Government Criminal Activity during the Rocky Flats Grand Jury Investigation.* New York: Apex Press, 2004.

William E. Loges and Jon Bruschke · *Free Press vs. Fair Trials: Examining Publicity's Role in Trial Outcomes.* London: Lawrence Erlbaum Associates, 2004.

Elayne Rapping · *Law and Justice as Seen on TV.* New York: New York University Press, 2003.

Albert R. Roberts · *Critical Issues in Crime and Justice.* Thousand Oaks, CA: Sage Publications, 2003.

Enika H. Schulze, Michael P. Jung, Rebecca P. Adams, et al. · *Introduction to the American Legal System.* Paramus, NJ: Prentice Hall, 2005.

Iris Teichmann · *Immigration and the Law.* Mankato, MN: Black Rabbit Books, 2006.

Jennifer Van Bergen	*The Twilight of Democracy: The Bush Plan for America.* Monroe, ME: Common Courage Press, 2004.
Bruce Wright	*Black Robes, White Justice: Why Our Legal System Doesn't Work for Blacks.* New York: Kensington Books, 2002.
John Yoo	*The Power of War and Peace: The Constitution and Foreign Affairs after 9/11.* Chicago: University of Chicago Press, 2005.

Index